Malaysian Kitchen

Malaysian Kitchen

Explore the exquisite food and cooking of Malaysia, with 80 superb recipes shown step by step in more than 350 beautiful photographs

Includes all the classic dishes from Hot and Sour Fish Soup and Mixed Seafood Hor Fun to Malay Lamb Korma and Mango and Lime Lassi

Ghillie Basan and Terry Tan

southwater

This edition is published by Southwater,
an imprint of Anness Publishing Ltd, Hermes House,
88–89 Blackfriars Road, London SE1 8HA;
tel. 020 7401 2077; fax 020 7633 9499

www.southwaterbooks.com; www.annesspublishing.com

If you like the images in this book and would like to investigate using them for publishing, promotions or advertising, please visit our website www.practicalpictures.com for more information.

UK distributor: Book Trade Services; tel. 0116 2759086; fax 0116 2759090; uksales@booktradeservices.com; exportsales@booktradeservices.comi
North American agent/distributor: National Book Network;
tel. 301 459 3366; fax 301 429 5746; www.nbnbooks.com
Australian agent/distributor: Pan Macmillan Australia;
tel. 1300 135 113; fax 1300 135 103; customer.service@macmillan.com.au
New Zealand agent/distributor: David Bateman Ltd;
tel. (09) 415 7664; fax (09) 415 8892

Publisher: Joanna Lorenz
Editorial Director: Helen Sudell
Project Editors: Rosie Gordon and Elizabeth Young
Home Economists: Lucy McKelvie, Bridget Sargeson and Fergal Connolly
Stylist: Helen Trent
Cover Design: Nigel Partridge
Page Design: Mike Morey
Proofreading Manager: Lindsay Zamponi
Production Controller: Christine Ni

Publisher's Acknowledgments

The publisher would like to thank William Lingwood and Martin Brigdale for their photography throughout the book, apart from the following images: istockphoto pp. 6b, 7t; Nicky Dowey p.16tc; Robert Harding Picture Library p.18; Superstock Ltd p.17t; Travel_ink pp. 9r, 10t, 10b, 11b, 13t, 14, 17b; Photoshot pp. 8b, 11t, 12, 13b, 15t, 15b, 16b, 19, 22.

A CIP catalogue record for this book is available from the British Library.

Previously published as part of a larger volume, *The Food and Cooking of Malaysia and Singapore*

Main front cover image shows Curry Kapitan with Coconut and Chilli Relish – for recipe, see page 74

Ethical Trading Policy

At Anness Publishing we believe that business should be conducted in an ethical and ecologically sustainable way, with respect for the environment and a proper regard to the replacement of the natural resources we employ.

As a publisher, we use a lot of wood pulp to make high-quality paper for printing, and that wood commonly comes from spruce trees. We are therefore currently growing more than 750,000 trees in three Scottish forest plantations: Berrymoss (130 hectares/320 acres), West Touxhill (125 hectares/305 acres) and Deveron Forest (75 hectares/185 acres). The forests we manage contain more than 3.5 times the number of trees employed each year in making paper for the books we manufacture.

Because of this ongoing ecological investment programme, you, as our customer, can have the pleasure and reassurance of knowing that a tree is being cultivated on your behalf to naturally replace the materials used to make the book you are holding.

Our forestry programme is run in accordance with the UK Woodland Assurance Scheme (UKWAS) and will be certified by the internationally recognized Forest Stewardship Council (FSC). The FSC is a non-government organization dedicated to promoting responsible management of the world's forests. Certification ensures forests are managed in an environmentally sustainable and socially responsible way. For further information about this scheme, go to www.annesspublishing.com/trees

Publisher's Note

Although the advice and information in this book are believed to be accurate and true at the time of going to press, neither the authors nor the publisher can accept any legal responsibility or liability for any errors or omissions that may be made nor for any inaccuracies nor for any loss, harm or injury that comes about from following instructions or advice in this book.

Notes

Bracketed terms are intended for American readers.

For all recipes, quantities are given in both metric and imperial measures and, where appropriate, in standard cups and spoons. Follow one set of measures, but not a mixture, because they are not interchangeable.

Standard spoon and cup measures are level. 1 tsp = 5ml, 1 tbsp = 15ml, 1 cup = 250ml/8fl oz.

Australian standard tablespoons are 20ml. Australian readers should use 3 tsp in place of 1 tbsp for measuring small quantities.

American pints are 16fl oz/2 cups. American readers should use 20fl oz/2.5 cups in place of 1 pint when measuring liquids.

Electric oven temperatures in this book are for conventional ovens. When using a fan oven, the temperature will probably need to be reduced by about 10–20°C/20–40°F. Since ovens vary, you should check with your manufacturer's instruction book for guidance.

The nutritional analysis given for each recipe is calculated per portion (i.e. serving or item), unless otherwise stated. If the recipe gives a range, such as Serves 4–6, then the nutritional analysis will be for the smaller portion size, i.e. 6 servings. Measurements for sodium do not include salt added to taste.

Medium (US large) eggs are used unless otherwise stated.

CONTENTS

INTRODUCTION

Malaysian food offers many tasty, gastronomical delights. The immense variety of dishes that can be found throughout Malaysia has been greatly influenced by its wonderfully multicultural population. The Chinese settlers imbued many a pot with their soy sauces and bean pastes, the legacy of which lives on in a hundred and one dishes in private homes, restaurants, food stalls and hawker complexes. These cooking methods have since drawn on the eclectic mix of the migrant Indian, Indonesian, Arab and European peoples.

THE IMPORTANCE OF SPICE

Blending spice and seasonings is an art that has evolved through centuries of multiculturalism. Malaysians have endlessly adventurous tastebuds and experimentation is vital to their kitchens. The keynote of the cuisine is spice paste, pounded rough or smooth, fried or boiled, rubbed on seafood or meat; each cook does his own fine-tuning to produce dishes of delectable character and taste. Within the Chinese communities, many dishes of the Cantonese, Hakka and Fujian – the three migrant mainstreams from South China – have retained their intrinsic purity, but some have embrace new flavours. A Fujian soy braised duck is touched with coriander and pepper, a Cantonese noodle dish is liberally spiced up with Indian chilli paste, and Malay desserts are given a fragrant fillip with sesame seeds – this is the beguiling culinary tableau.

Sour Nonya curries rely on the staple tamarind base that typifies Indonesian seafood dishes; meat and poultry cuts are bathed in redolent sambals that speak of South Indian heat; staple rice and noodles from Guangzhou province are flavoured with myriad tropical herbs largely unused in China; and countless cakes and sweet concoctions are spun out of coconut, palm sugar and glutinous rice.

The subtle or robust flavours of Chinese stir-fries take on piquant highlights in the Malay kitchen; for

Above: Malaysian spring rolls, known as Chuen Piah, are a speciality of Penang cooking. They are wrapped in bean curd instead of flour wrappers.

Below: A colourful and bustling morning market full of a variety of fresh fruits and vegetables in Kota Bharu, located in the city of Kelantan, Malaysia.

example, Chinese chicken dishes may be perfumed with indigenous herbs such as coriander and lemon grass. Coconut milk – the dairy equivalent in the region – is the liquid basis for many a hybrid creation, reflecting Indonesian, Thai and Indian culinary touches to all types of food.

A COOKS' HAVEN

Whether in the relaxed ambience of Malaysian villages or the pulsating rhythm of urban life in the cities, food remains the foundation of daily life. Rich aromas fragrance the air, the coastal areas are teeming with marine life and there has always been an abundance of seafood and river catches. Local rice has the best textures, there are bountiful wild and farmed fruit harvests, and of course there is the wonderful herb garden that is Malaysia's natural heritage. The reputation for incomparable culinary skills among Malaysian cooks has not been earned consciously; it seems inherited by the people from their ingenious and inventive ancestors. Successive generations have adapted, improved and refined dishes, creating a rainbow palette of flavours. Of all the world's cuisines, this is one of the least intimidating, and yet the most rewarding. Dishes vary depending on which state, town, village and ethnic community it comes from. While the

village lifestyle of old is rapidly being left in the past, and the faster pace of city life means that people have less time, the core of Malaysian food remains sacrosanct. Whether it is a banquet of a dozen dishes, a lunch or dinner of just a few simple dishes, or snacks from street vendors, visitors to any area will discover that eating is a national obsession.

Above: Fishing villages can be found all along the coasts of Malaysia. Most fishermen go out in the early hours of the night and return around dawn.

ABOUT THIS BOOK

Perhaps you have visited Malaysia and long to relive the tastes and scents of the food you ate there, or have enjoyed a Malaysian meal in a restaurant. Alternatively, you may enjoy Thai or Indian food and want to discover related cuisines. Whatever the case, you will find the information in this book offers a fascinating insight into the history and people behind the food.

The recipes aim to immerse you in the true experience of Malaysia's food, with classic soups and broths, noodle and rice dishes, exotic desserts, and a fiery selection of meat, poultry and fish and shellfish dishes.

The selection of dishes featured in this book shows how to make the most out of the fresh ingredients available, as well as store-cupboard staples, and are easy to prepare quickly and enjoy at leisure with friends and family. Above all, they introduce new experiences; from shopping in bustling food markets to the tantalizing cooking smells and unforgettable flavours of the final meal.

Below: Rice is cooked in many delicious ways in Malaysia.

Below: Sweet-flavoured lassi is widely drunk in coffee shops and restaurants.

A CULINARY HISTORY
OF MALAYSIA

The independent country of Malaysia as we know it today only emerged in the 1960s. Malaysia was born in 1963, with the merging of Malaya, Singapore, Sabah and Sarawak, while the small sultanate of Brunei in north Borneo remained separate. However, Singapore's merger into Malaysia soon proved an unhappy one. Singapore broke free in 1965 and has since then succeeded spectacularly well as a small nation, with an emphasis on hard work and a tight economy.

For centuries before their emergence as independent nations, however, the influxes of traders, colonialists and immigrant workers had been adding to the rich cultural melting-pot that now characterizes these two countries. The cultural mix of Malaysia is so diverse that it reads like a recipe in itself. The population of Malaysia is about 60 per cent Malay, 26 per cent Chinese and 7 per cent Indian, with a dash of Peranakan, Eurasian, Indonesian and tribal influences, garnished with a scattering of Vietnamese, Japanese, Filipino and Thai. Most Malays are followers of Islam, as well as adhering to old spiritual beliefs and systems of social law. In the *kampung* (Malay village), the early Hindu-based system of *adat*, with an emphasis on collective responsibility, is part of everyday life. Obligations of kinship and social harmony are at the heart of the Malay psyche, so much so that many urban Malays, caught up in the busy whirl of Kuala Lumpur, miss the spiritual simplicity of *kampung* life.

There are two distinct parts of Malaysia, which are separated by the South China Sea. Both areas share a landscape that features coastal plains with lush forests and mountains. The official capital and largest city is Kuala Lumpur, which is an international shopping destination and home to many street markets selling regional food. Malaysia has many natural resources, especially in agriculture. It is one of the top exporters of palm oil, cocoa, pepper, pineapple and tobacco.

Above: Modern-day Malaysia is divided into the two distinct regions of West and East, covering 329,758 sq km/ 127,320 sq miles. West Malaysia (the Malay Peninsula) is joined to mainland Asia with Singapore at the bottom. East Malaysia encompasses the northern part of Borneo and is divided into two states, Sabah and Sarawak.

Above: The busy Johur Bakra causeway links Singapore to Malaysia.

MALAYAN ANCESTRY

The Orang Asli, the aboriginal Malays, provide us with the most vivid evidence as to early Malay culinary culture. They are believed to have migrated 10,000 years ago from the region in China where the great rivers of South-east Asia meet (today's Qinghai Province). The Orang Asli settled in the forests of the Malay Peninsula, where they led a hunter-gatherer existence. Their numbers dwindled considerably during the 20th century, and some have intermarried with other ethnic groups in the region, but there are still pockets of hunter-gatherer Orang Asli living in the hilly jungles of Pahang in the centre of the peninsula.

Other Malay descendants who settled on the peninsula were said to be of the same ethnic group as their Indonesian ancestors. Culturally they were similar, particularly when it came to food and culinary traditions: this common bond still exists, as the Malays and Indonesians share many of the same spicy dishes. As the Malay ancestors settled on the peninsula, some moved inland and married Orang Asli tribespeople, spreading their knowledge of rice cultivation and the use of the ox and water buffalo as beasts of burden.

Over in East Malaysia, Sabah and Sarawak are still home to numerous indigenous tribal groups, who continue

Right: A traditional fishing boat tied up on the fine sands of Penang, on Malaysia's west coast.

to live by fishing, hunting and collecting wild plants and herbs, most of which are indigenous to those regions.

THE STORY OF MELAKA

A turning point in the region's culinary history came at around 1400, when the small fishing village of Melaka on the west coast of the Malay Peninsula began to grow into a significant port. With Indian ships sailing in on the southwest monsoon and Chinese junks being blown in by the north west monsoon, Melaka was strategically positioned to harbour them and boomed as a multicultural trade centre, drawing traders, merchants and missionaries to its shores.

The local cooking was influenced by the arrival of new cooking techniques, spices such as cardamom, pepper and cloves, and exotic fruits and vegetables. When the Sultan of Melaka converted to Islam in the mid-15th century, there was an increase in trade with other

Above: Spices grown locally add unmistakable warmth, sweetness and flavour to the region's food.

Muslim communities in Indonesia and the Middle East, which had a lasting effect on Malay cuisine.

Melaka's colourful history has left it an enviable culinary heritage. Malay, Chinese, Peranakan and Eurasian cuisines all flourish, and many local recipes put a particular emphasis on spices and creamy coconut milk. The sago pudding soaked in palm sugar syrup, *sagu gula melaka*, is a Malay favourite, as is *satay celup*, an assortment of skewered food such as shellfish, vegetables, fish balls, hard-boiled quail's eggs and chunks of chicken or beef, which is cooked in boiling stock, rather like a Swiss fondue, and served with a peanut sauce. Satay is likely to have evolved from the Middle Eastern kebab, which would have been brought to the region by Muslim Indian or Arab traders.

Right: A stall holder tends his wares in Batu Ferringhi in Penang. Malaysian produce is now widely exported.

PENANG

Off the mainland, the small island of Penang grew as a major trade centre under the rule of the British East India Company in the 18th and 19th centuries, when it was one of the best sources of nutmeg and cloves. At this time it attracted immigrants from China, Sumatra, Thailand, Burma and India. The intermingling of these varied cultures is reflected in the food of Penang, which is regarded as a gastronomic heaven.

INDIA'S INFLUENCE

Traders from India had visited the region long before Europeans set up colonies. However, it was not until the 19th century, when the British brought

Below: Water buffalo are a common sight on Longwaki Island, and are used as beasts of burden as well as for food.

in Indian workers to provide cheap labour in the rubber plantations, that Indian culture had a strong influence on the cuisine of the region. Most of these Indians were Hindus from South India, where rice and dhal (lentils) are the staples, and food is eaten with the

hands. Hindus don't eat beef and many are vegetarian, so they introduced vegetable dishes and pickles to Malay cuisine. Southern Indians also tend to cook with coconut oil, contrasting with the ghee-based dishes of North India, such as *tandoori* and *biryani*.

Above: A fish market scene at Kota Bharu in Kelantan.

CHINESE FLAVOURS

Like the Indians, the Chinese had had a long history of trade in the region, but it wasn't until the 19th century that the resident Chinese population grew. With the increase in the region's tin mining and agriculture, the numbers of Chinese grew so quickly that, by 1827, they formed the largest single community in Singapore. By 1845, they made up half the population. Tremendous farmers, the Chinese were responsible for planting many of the rice paddies and vegetable plantations in the region.

Hailing from the provinces of Guangdong, Fujian and Guangxi, they belonged to different socio-linguistic groups, such as Teochew, Hokkien and Hainanese, each of which adheres to its own traditions and cuisines.

EURASIAN HYBRID COOKING

In the 16th century, Portuguese traders and explorers colonized parts of Malaysia, particularly Melaka, and married local women. The descendants called themselves Jenti Cristang

Right: A Chinese market at Penang, known as the "Pearl of the Orient".

(Christian people) and spoke their own language, a kind of Creole Portuguese. They were also called Eurasian, along with the descendants of other European-Malay unions, and developed their own cuisine, a complex hybrid of Malay, Chinese, Peranakan and Indian food, combined with Portuguese cooking methods. The European influence in this food can be detected in their love of roasted cuts of meat, grilled chops and steaks. However, exotic curries, with sour notes of tamarind and lime, are also Eurasian top favourites, including the fiery curry *debal* (devil's curry) and *feng*, the Christmas pork curry. Curries and other savoury dishes are usually served with rice or bread but, unlike the other culinary cultures of Malaysia and Singapore, the Eurasians enjoy a dessert at the end of a meal.

MALAYSIAN CUISINE TODAY

The rich variety of culinary traditions found throughout South-east Asia come together in Malaysia. From Chinese businessmen in skyscrapers in Kuala Lumpur to Orang Asli hunter-gatherers in the jungles of the Malay Peninsula, the people and their eating habits are as diverse as the landscape. Thanks to its location on the sea routes between Asia, India and China, Malaysia has been influenced by merchants and invaders from far and wide.

OUTSIDE INFLUENCES

Bordering Thailand to the north, the states of Perlis and Kedah are known as the region's rice bowl, producing over half the domestic rice supply. Given its proximity to Thailand and the influx of Thais settling in the region, the local cuisine is inevitably influenced by the Thai culinary trademark – hot, spicy flavours paired with sourness.

Further down the west coast, in the states of Perak and Selangor and in the capital, Kuala Lumpur, the food is much more varied, influenced in succession by Indian traders, Chinese merchants, European colonizers, immigrant workers and 20th-century industrialization. Kuala Lumpur, which has grown from a

Above: A modern satay stall in Kuala Lumpar, Malaysia, where street snacking is extremely popular.

19th-century tin-mining town to an affluent, cosmopolitan city, boasts a fascinating mélange of food cultures. You can find regional specialities from all parts of Malaysia as well as from India and China; you can sample French, Vietnamese and Japanese fare in high-class restaurants; seek out old colonial haunts serving British breakfasts and fried chicken with Worcestershire sauce; or simply follow the young crowd and wait at a busy hawker stall for a bowl of noodles with a fried egg on top.

STRONGHOLDS OF TRADITION

Much of Malaysia's tea is grown on the plantations in Perak's highlands, which lead into the Cameron Highlands of Pahang. The area's fertile plateaux attracted tea planters, vegetable farmers and wealthy colonialists retreating from the heat of the lowlands to highland hill stations. However, much of Pahang has remained impenetrable to prospectors and planters, dividing the east and west of the Malaysian peninsula with its high mountain ridges. This is the domain of the indigenous Orang Asli, whose staple foods are tapioca, rice and fish. Malaysia's longest river, Sungai Pahang, flows right through the state and is full of plump carp and catfish.

Over on the east coast, the states of Kelantan and Terengganu are still steeped in traditional Malay culture. The coastline is dotted with thriving fishing villages and idyllic white beaches. Life moves at a slower pace, with fishing as its mainstay. Fish is bought from the nets as the boats come to shore and the local women cook it in inventive ways.

In the south of the peninsula, Negeri Sembilan is known for seriously fiery dishes, influenced by the Minangkabau, who came from Sumatra in the 15th century. The most southerly state on the peninsula is Johor, which has also retained a strong Malay culture and cuisine. Johor provides the crowded island of Singapore with much of its farm produce and water. Linked to Singapore by two causeways, Johor Bahru, the state capital, offers much of the same hawker food, and

Singaporeans often drive over to Johor Bahru to eat cheaper versions of their own delicious seafood dishes.

EAST MALAYSIA

Across the South China Sea, most visitors to Sabah on the island of Borneo go to climb Mount Kinabalu or visit the orang-utan rehabilitation centre. However, Sabah is also home to gorgeous deserted beaches, coral reefs and wild Asian elephants and rhinos, as well as to 30 different ethnic groups who thrive on a diet of fish, deer, wild boar and wild plants, herbs and fruit from the forests. Although rice is grown in the hills, the main staples for the indigenous communities are corn, tapioca (cassava) and, in the swamp lands, pearls from the wild sago palm.

Like Sabah, Sarawak is a world apart from the Malay Peninsula. Covered with dense rainforests, rivers, caves and national parks where wildlife can be spotted, this state is home to the Iban, Melanau and other indigenous tribes. Longhouses and river excursions through the jungles using old head-hunter trails are part of the tourist experience, as is the city of Kuching. Although rice is grown in Sarawak, vast areas of the land are too swampy for paddies, so some tribes rely on the wild sago palm. Wild boar and deer are Sarawakan favourites, roasted whole over charcoal. Most tribes make their own arak, a local liquor, and tuak, rice wine, which are both very potent.

COFFEE SHOP CULTURE

Malaysian coffee shops are friendly and atmospheric. Often occupying the ground floors of old city shophouses, the setup is basic, with minimal decoration and plain tables and chairs. Each neighbourhood has its own Chinese, Malay or Indian coffee shop, where people gather for a chat and a cup of tea or coffee and, frequently, a meal. Meals served in coffee shops are simple and culture-specific, such as the fish head soup served in the Indian and Malay premises, or noodles and dim sum in the Chinese shops. For breakfast, popular choices include *roti kaya* (grilled flatbread smeared with coconut egg jam) and *kuay neng* (runny, soft-boiled eggs cracked open in a saucer and mixed with soy sauce and black pepper).

Tea is generally Assam, made strong and sweetened with condensed milk. Frothy *teh tarik* ("pulled tea") is a Malaysian speciality, and the warm, milky ginger tea known as *teh halia* is regarded as a late-night pick-me-up. Chinese jasmine or lotus teas are served to enhance the appetite, cleanse the blood or aid digestion, but coffee begins and ends the day for many Malays. Brewed strong with earthy and mellow characteristics, it is always sweetened with condensed milk.

Right: Fishing nets dry outside a small house in Kampung, Malaysia. In some areas the traditional ways of life are almost unchanged.

How eateries have changed

Throughout Malaysia there are still many terraced "shophouses" dating back to the years before World War II, with the living quarters upstairs and the ground floor devoted to a small business. Many were turned into eating houses or coffee shops as street hawkers gradually left the streets and started selling their noodles and rice dishes from these small premises. It is a trade that has remained largely unchanged in most urban areas.

In Penang, Ipoh, Malacca, Seremban and villages along the east coast, and in the East Malaysian states of Sawarak and Sabah, coffee shops retain their pre-war ambience, serving basic and inexpensive dishes such as noodles, rice with a plethora of curries, stir-fried seafood and snacks such as curry puffs, Indian breads and other homely offerings.

In other parts of the country many of these coffee houses were abandoned and left to decay, but in recent decades their potential as tourist attractions has been realized.

In Kuala Lumpur, for instance, they have been air-conditioned and made more up-market, with prices to match. Their distinctive marble-topped tables and black bentwood chairs have now become a décor hallmark throughout Malaysia, emulated by interior designers furnishing luxury flats.

Above: The cityscape of Kuala Lumpur indicates this luxurious era.

At the same time there has been an upsurge of shopping complexes in major towns. These invariably feature a "food court", with formerly itinerant street hawkers housed in sparkling new premises. Restaurants from out-of-town areas have also opted to open establishments in these complexes, and they mark a definite change in eating habits among the locals. For Malaysians as well as tourists, they have become comfort zones to escape from the unyielding heat and humidity.

Most menus are still traditional, and serious foodies can find all their favourite dishes, but there are also the Western fast food counters with burgers and pizzas, patronized mainly by younger people. You can see the writing on the wall: it's only a matter of time before the old eating houses go the way of history, to be replaced by food courts with all the benefits of luxury living and dining. But for the moment Malaysia still has much to offer to visitors and locals looking for a traditional experience.

REGIONAL FLAVOURS

The people of Malaysia are proud of their diverse culinary cultures and regional food. In the cities you can eat just about anything, from traditional Hainanese chicken rice to contemporary chilli crab. At the heart and soul of Malay food is the *rempah*, a spicy mixture made by first pounding wet ingredients such as shallots, ginger, garlic and chilli, and then adding dry spices such as coriander seeds, cardamom and ground turmeric, to form a paste. This mixture is then cooked in oil before any of the other ingredients of the dish are added.

Rice is the basis of many traditional Malay meals, either cooked plain or flavoured with coconut milk or spices. Traditional rice dishes include *ketupat* (pressed rice cooked in coconut fronds) and *lemang* (rice stuffed into hollow bamboo tubes lined with banana leaves and cooked over a charcoal fire). Generally, a Malay meal consists of a fish or shellfish curry or a meat or chicken dish, served with rice, a vegetable dish and a chilli sambal. Bread is often served instead of rice, particularly with dishes in which there is lots of richly flavoured sauce that begs to be mopped up with chunks of fresh, crusty baguette. The Malays also enjoy the Indian flat, flaky bread, *roti paratha*, with curries. They also often eat it as a snack, sprinkled with sugar. Each group eats the same foods in slightly different ways, adjusting the balance to suit their taste, such as the Malay desire for a chilli kick with every mouthful. In rural Malaysia the food is more regionalized.

LOCAL SPECIALITIES

In Kedah and Perlis in the north of the Malay Peninsula, the Thai influence is evident. The fishermen and rice farmers of these two states favour simple fish dishes, flavoured with chillies, lemon grass, kaffir lime leaves, lime juice and fish sauce. These are often tempered with a sweet prawn (shrimp) sauce, *otak udang*, and served with herbs and shredded cucumber.

Ipoh is well known for its authentic Chinese food, introduced by the immigrant population that worked in the tin mines; Penang and Melaka are famed for their delicious Nonya dishes; and Kelantan is regarded as pure Malay.

It boasts some unique specialities, such as *nasi dagang* (glutinous rice cooked in coconut milk and served with fish, grated coconut, herbs and sauces), the famous *nasi kerabu*, a rice dish tinted blue with dye from the pea flower, and *bunga telang*, which is served with fish crackers and fried salted fish.

In Terengganu, the savoury pastries, *epok-epok*, are filled with fish and grated coconut, and the local delicacy, *satar*, is made by stuffing banana-leaf cones with a spicy-sour fish paste and grilling them over charcoal. The Malay speciality, *rendang* (beef cooked in coconut milk), is held to be best in Negeri Sembilan, where it is served with *lemang*, glutinous rice cooked with coconut milk inside bamboo poles positioned over a fire.

In Johor, a local speciality is *satay Johor*, in which skewered meat is continuously basted with a mixture of coconut milk and oil, brushed on with a lemon grass stalk, which imparts a delicate flavour. *Laksa Johor* is also popular: noodles in coconut milk are served with chunks of herring and flavoured with tamarind and mint.

THE TRIBES OF SABAH

Borneo is home to an astonishing number of animal species as well as tribal peoples whose way of life hardly seems to have changed with the centuries. In Sabah, the northernmost state, there are some 30 tribes, speaking 50 or more dialects and languages. Sabah has a huge diversity of ethnic groups who have settled there over hundreds of years and adapted their eating styles to the local habitat. The Kadazans, the main tribal community in the west, favour the sour tastes of unripe mangoes, limes and tangy star fruit and are particularly proud of their fish dish, *hinava tongii*, which combines fresh mackerel with

Left: The dense and fertile Cameron Highlands in Pahang have attracted thousands of planters and farmers and, as a result, vegetable crops, flowers and tea bushes still grow in profusion in the plateaux and on the foothills.

Left: Childen of the Orang Asli tribe In Taman Negara, Malaysia.

PENANG: GASTRONOMIC HEAVEN

The varied cuisine of Penang has led to its acclaim as Malaysia's food capital. Specialities of the island include the Indian-inspired *murtabak*, flatbread filled with spicy minced (ground) beef or lamb and vegetables; Peranakan *pasembur*, a salad of yam, bean, tofu, cuttlefish and cucumber tossed with beansprouts and prawn (shrimp) fritters in a sweet and sour dressing; Penang *asam laksa*, the local noodles in coconut milk, with flakes of mackerel, garnished with pineapple, cucumber, chilli, mint and shrimp paste; and *pong piah*, a Hokkien dish of flaky pastry filled with milky syrup.

The Indian coffee shops in Penang are also famous for their pulled tea, *teh tarik*, which is deliciously sweet and frothy. It is usually made by a man, who pours the sweetened tea from a metal pot held above his head into another one held below his waist and repeats the process several times until a layer of froth has formed on the surface and the tea has cooled to drinking temperature, when it is poured into the cup. Also known descriptively as *teh terbang*, or "flying tea", it is an acquired skill, and a spectacle that is just as popular with the locals as it is with tourists.

Below: Penang harbour's ragged stilt houses are the gateway to a "gastronomic heaven".

chillies, ginger, shallots and lime juice and one special ingredient that makes all the difference – the grated stone (pit) of a local mango, the bambangan. Dried shrimps and anchovies are added to many dishes.

Sabah's national fish dish, *hinava*, consists of finely sliced raw fish marinated in lime juice and herbs.

The Bisaya, a Muslim group, use the sago to make a thick porridge, *ambuyat*, which they dip into a fiery sambal. In the hilly south-west, the Murut hunt wild boar, chop up the meat and stuff it, with chunks of freshwater fish, jungle leaves, rice grains and salt, into the hollow of bamboo stems, where the mixture is left to ferment for weeks, even months. This pungent speciality, *jaruk*, is eaten with steamed rice or tapioca. A local beverage, rice wine, or *tapai*, is made from glutinous rice and yeast, and is enjoyed by the non-Muslim Sabahan tribespeople. The Murut are traditionally rice and tapioca (cassava) farmers, but are recently expanding to cultivate vegetables, such as aubergines (eggplants) and spinach. Tropical plants and fruits provide spice and sweetness to their cooking.

THE JUNGLES OF SARAWAK

Like Sabah, Sarawak is a world apart from the Malaysian peninsula. Covered with dense rainforests, rivers, caves and national parks, this state is home to the Dayaks, Ibans, Melanau and other indigenous tribes. Longhouses and river excursions through the jungles using head-hunter trails are part of the tourist experience, as is the city of Kuching. Although rice is grown in Sarawak, vast areas of the land are too swampy for paddies, so some tribes rely on the wild sago palm for carbohydrate. A Melanau fisherman's dish, *umai*, consists of finely sliced raw fish, marinated in tamarind or lime juice with chopped shallots, chillies and salt, and served with a bowl of toasted sago pearls. In Sabah the sago pearls are boiled to make a porridge-like paste, usually eaten with a fiery sambal. Sago grubs (young caterpillars found in sago palms) are also popular among tribal peoples.

Wild boar and deer are Sarawakan favourites, roasted whole over charcoal, or used for satay dishes, accompanied by vegetable dishes. Most tribes make their own arak, a local liquor, and tuak, rice wine, which are very potent.

NONYA CUISINE

When the early Chinese traders began to settle in the ports of Penang and Melaka from the 15th century onward, a number of them married local Malay women to create an ethnic sub-group of Malay-Chinese. In Malay, this group is called Peranakan, which means "half caste", but they also refer to themselves as Straits Chinese to distinguish themselves from the Chinese immigrant workers who came to the Malay Peninsula later.

Using the Peranakan words for male (*baba*) and female (*nonya*), this group was also referred to as the Baba-Nonyas, and was noted for its distinctive dress, lavishly decorated homes and, above all, for its cuisine. The Peranakans were relatively wealthy,

so they were able to indulge in elaborate meals that were an inspired mix of Chinese and Malay traditions. As the food was prepared by the women, it became known as Nonya cuisine.

To this day, the unique Nonya cooking is highly praised and much sought after, with its lavish use of chillies, lemon grass, galangal and turmeric fused with elements of Indian, Thai, Portuguese and Chinese cooking methods. Classic Nonya dishes include *mee siam*, a Thai-influenced dish of rice noodles in a spicy, tangy sauce, and

Left: A street food vendor fanning the flames at a satay stall.

Below: Pulau Pertentian in Malaysia is one of many unspoilt beauty spots.

babi pong tey, a pork stew cooked in an earthenware pot. It is worth looking out for Nonya *tok panjang*, which translates as "Nonya long table". It consists of an elaborate buffet spread of Nonya specialities. The style of eating is similar to Malay, as most dishes are served with rice or bread and are accompanied by a chilli sambal or a bowl of fiery chillies.

INDIAN AND CHINESE STALLS

The most distinctive style of Indian cooking is that found at the *mamak* (Indian Muslim) hawker stalls, where the cooks combine the wondrous Malay and Indian flavours and traditional cooking techniques. The resulting spicy dishes are in a class of their own, such as *mee rebus* (thick, fresh, egg noodles in a sweet, spicy sauce served with eggs and chillies) and *rojak* (a crispy vegetable salad with fried tofu and fish cakes in a spicy-sweet sauce). A feature of Indian food that stands out from the rest is the use of yogurt as a cooling accompaniment to hot curries, either served plain, or mixed with vegetables and herbs in a *raita* or *pachadi*, or blended in *lassi*, a popular refreshing yogurt drink.

Traditionally, rice has always been the staple of Chinese cooking. The Chinese do not waste any part of any living

Above: A typical Malaysian open air market, full of colour.

Below: Women in Langkawi harvest the rice crops in the traditional way.

creature, and rice can be served with anything from duck's feet, to dog, to sea cucumber. The Chinese communities of Malaysia still eat much the same as their ancestors, based on the principles of yin and yang: sweet and sour, hot and cold, plain and spicy.

The Indian and Malay influence has in turn made an impact on some of the traditional Chinese dishes, particularly those served at hawker stalls. Spicy favourites include *char kway teow*, stir-fried rice noodles with prawns (shrimp), squid and Chinese sausage, and Hainanese chicken rice, which is served with a dish of chillies on the side to satisfy the Malay taste for hot spicy flavours. A legacy of the 19th-century colonial period, when the British acquired Malaya, is the addition of Western ingredients. The British "cookboys" were generally Hainanese, so tomato ketchup and Worcestershire sauce appear among the more conventional ingredients of some of the Chinese dishes.

CELEBRATIONS AND FESTIVALS

With such a variety of culinary cultures, every religious or family celebration is a banquet of delights. Traditional weddings involve a great deal of feasting, some of which is symbolic and can span several days. Throughout Malaysia, births also require ceremonial feasting, which often takes place on the 100th day of the child's life in Chinese and Peranakan households. Special foods are called for at Chinese New Year, the Muslim Hari Raya Puasa, Indian Diwali, Christmas and other festivals.

WEDDINGS

At Malay weddings, the feasting is on a huge scale, with hundreds of guests who must be served a selection of rice dishes and curries. As they depart, each guest is presented with delicately wrapped gifts of hard-boiled eggs to ensure fertility for the newlyweds. Indian weddings also operate on a large scale, with a vast selection of dishes tailored to the various religious and regional groups, such as Bengalis, Punjabis and Tamils, attending.

Chinese weddings are more restrained, with a traditional tea ceremony and a family banquet. On an auspicious day, the groom visits the bride's house to pay his respects and ask for her hand. When accepted, the groom and his bride return to his home, where they kneel before his parents and older relatives and serve them a specially brewed tea to symbolize that the bride will undertake her new role of serving and caring for her in-laws. The final banquet is usually supplied by the groom's parents, who take traditional gifts of food, such as a suckling pig, to be eaten at the bride's house.

In a Peranakan marriage, the bride's future mother-in-law traditionally cooks a special coconut rice dish, *nasi lemak*, which she takes as a symbolic offering to the bride's mother to reassure her that the bride is still a virgin.

CHRISTMAS

The snow that traditionally accompanies Christmas in northern Europe may not appear in Malaysia, but there is no shortage of fake snow, twinkling lights, furs, shiny baubles and silver tinsel. Christmas may be a Eurasian festival, but everyone joins in, from the decorations to the presents and feasting. In Eurasian households, it is common to find roast turkey on the Christmas table – stuffed with glutinous rice, pork and chestnuts. Honey-baked hams keep up the Western tradition, but are often accompanied by chicken or pork curries, such as curry *debal* and *feng*, which is made a day in advance to enhance the flavour. With such a colourful European and Malay heritage, the Eurasians draw from all their different influences at Christmas, adding soy-based dishes, chilli dips, steamed cabbage rolls, fruit cakes and sponge cakes to the feast. As most Eurasians are Catholic, they attend midnight mass on Christmas Eve and return home to a table laden with festive delicacies.

CHINESE NEW YEAR

Shortly after Christmas, preparations for the Chinese New Year begin. Traditionally, this festival marked the advent of spring for the Chinese farmers, but for the largely urban Chinese population the event represents a spiritual renewal rather than a physical one. Houses are cleaned, debts settled, new clothes bought and gifts of money exchanged. On New Year's Day, orange segments are presented to guests for good fortune, and sweets (candy) and cakes are offered to ensure a sweet future.

Left: A traditional wedding feast of local fruits and specialities laid out before a newly-married Hindu couple.

In Malaysia, a Peranakan New Year meal usually includes a wide range of traditional food, such as chicken cooked in a tamarind sauce, and the streets are bustling with hawkers selling bak kwa – a salty-sweet dried meat.

HARI RAYA PUASA

The third major festival on the calendar is the Muslim Hari Raya Puasa, which marks the end of Ramadan, the month of fasting and abstaining from other sensory pleasures between dawn and dusk. For the men, the day begins with prayers in the mosques; they then go on to the cemeteries to pay their respects to dead relatives. The women are busy preparing food, cakes, sweets, biscuits, and other delicacies that they will sere on the day of Hari Raya. The feast will usually include *rendang* (beef cooked in coconut milk), which is served with *ketupat* (compressed rice cakes) and *serunding*, a side dish of grated coconut fried with chilli. Once this meal is over,

friends and family visit one another, bearing gifts of food, cakes and sweetmeats, which are enjoyed with tea and coffee or syrupy drinks. The celebrations sometimes carry on into the night with the lighting of home-made firecrackers.

DIWALI

The Festival of Lights, Diwali, is a Hindu celebration, marking the triumph of good over evil. It takes place on the rising of the new moon in the seventh month of the Hindu calendar, when oil lamps and candles are lit to welcome Lakshmi, the goddess of wealth. To celebrate the occasion, a wonderful array of spicy vindaloo and biryani dishes, flatbreads and chutneys are prepared for gatherings of friends and relatives.

GAWAI DAYAK

In Sarawak, the Dayak (the collective name for all the tribes of the area) celebrate the end of the rice harvest

Above: Chinese New Year celebrations involve colourful processions and special feasts.

with a festival, Gawai Dayak. Feasts and a ceremony to cast out the spirit of greediness commence on 31st May, and continue overnight into 1st June. Preparations, cooking and fermenting wine starts well in advance, and on Gawai eve, glutinous rice is roasted in bamboo. The communities celebrate this festival, with a great deal of merry-making and dancing, enhanced by the home-brewed rice wine, tuak.

Cockfights, war dances and blow pipe competitions are all part of the festivities, which are rounded off with local delicacies, such as *ikan kasam* (fermented fish stir-fried with black beans) and a touch more alcohol in the fermented durian pulp, *tempoyak*.

At this time many Dayak weddings take place, as it is the only occasion when so many people get together.

TRADITIONAL EQUIPMENT

The traditional Southeast Asian kitchen is basic. Often dark and sparsely kitted out with an open hearth, very little equipment is needed. Food is generally bought daily from the markets, taken home and cooked immediately, so unless you visit the kitchen during the frenzied moments of activity over the hearth, there is little evidence of food or cooking in homes.

In the days when there were no refrigerators, the reliance on fresh produce from the daily markets was vital. For some, two visits to the market were required – in the morning for the ingredients to cook for lunch, and in the afternoon for the evening meal.

Back in the kitchen, the activity begins with the scrubbing of vegetables, the plucking and jointing of birds (if it hasn't been done in the markets), endless chopping and slicing, and the pounding of herbs and spices with a mortar and pestle.

WOK

The wok is the most important utensil for everyday cooking and everybody has one. Without a doubt, there is always something delicious being stir-fried in a home or in the streets. However, woks are not only used for stir-frying, they are also used for steaming, deep-frying, braising and soup-making. The most functional, multi-purpose wok should measure approximately 35cm/14in across, large enough for a family meal or to steam a whole fish. The most common wok is double-handled and made of lightweight carbonized steel. This is ideal for deep-frying and steaming but, for stir-frying, you need the single-handled version.

When you first buy a wok, you need to season it before use. Put it over a high heat to blacken the inside – this burns off any dust and factory coating. Leave the wok to cool, then immerse it in hot, soapy water and clean it with an abrasive cloth or stiff brush. Rinse it well and dry over a medium heat. Pour a little cooking oil into the base and, using kitchen paper, wipe all around the surface of the wok. Now the wok is ready for use.

After each use, clean the wok with hot water only, dry it over a medium heat, and wipe a thin layer of oil over the surface. This will ensure that it doesn't get rusty.

Above: A solid mortar and pestle is an essential piece of kitchen equipment.

MORTAR AND PESTLE

A big mortar and pestle, made of stone, is of particular value, as it is used not only for grinding spices, chillies and garlic, but also for pounding all the condiments and pastes, as well as the meat for pâtés and savoury balls. Some cooks have several mortar and pestle sets, varying in size according to the activity and ingredient. Coffee grinders and electric blenders can be used as substitutes, but they don't release the oils and flavours of the ingredients in the same way and they produce too smooth a texture. It is worth looking for a solid stone mortar and pestle in Asian markets and kitchen suppliers.

BAMBOO STEAMER

Traditional bamboo steamers come in various sizes. The most practical one is about 30cm/12in wide, as it can be used for rice or a whole fish. Generally, the steamer is set directly over a wok that is filled with boiling water to below the level of the steamer. The food is placed in the steamer, either on a plate, or wrapped in muslin (cheesecloth), or banana leaves. The lid is placed on the steamer and, as the water in the wok is heated, the steam rises under and around the food, cooking it gently. A stainless steel steamer is no substitute for a bamboo one, which imparts its

Left: A single-handled wok is good for stir-frying; a double-handled wok is better for steaming and deep-frying.

own delicate fragrance to the dish. Bamboo steamers are available in most Asian stores and some cooking equipment suppliers.

CHOPSTICKS

For cooking, look for long chopsticks made from bamboo. Chopsticks are used to eat with, as well as for cooking, though Malaysian food is often eaten with the hand (always the right hand). Following Chinese methods, many cooks will use a set of long chopsticks for stirring, mixing, tasting, and as tongs. Eating chopsticks are traditionally made from bamboo or wood, but more elaborate ones can be made from ivory, bone, gold, silver or jade.

CLAY POT

Made from a combination of light-coloured clay and sand, these pots come in all sizes, with single or double handles, lids, and glazed interiors.

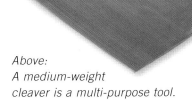

Above: A clay pot can be used in the oven or, with care, on the stove.

Right: Bamboo steamers come in several sizes.

Perhaps the oldest form of cooking vessel, these attractive pots are ideal for slow-cooking, braised dishes and soups, as they retain an overall even heat. Generally, they are used on the stove over a low or medium heat, as a high temperature could cause a crack. When you first buy a clay pot, it needs to be treated for cooking. Fill it with water and place it over a low flame, then gradually increase the heat and let the water boil until it is reduced by half. Rinse the pot and dry it thoroughly. Now it is ready for use. Traditional clay pots are available in some Asian markets.

Left: Bamboo chopsticks are essential kitchen equipment.

*Above:
A medium-weight cleaver is a multi-purpose tool.*

CLEAVERS

Asian cleavers are the most important tools in the kitchen. There are special blades for the fine chopping of lemon grass and green papaya, heavy blades for opening coconuts, thin ones for shredding spring onions (scallions), and multi-purpose ones for any type of chopping, slicing and crushing. Generally, you use the front, lighter part of the blade for the regular chopping, slicing and shredding; the back, heavier section is for chopping with force through bones; and the flat side is ideal for crushing ginger and garlic, and for transporting ingredients into the wok.

DRAINING SPOONS

Traditional draining spoons are made of wire and have a long bamboo handle; more modern ones are made completely of stainless steel with a perforated spoon. Both are flat and extremely useful for deep-frying, for blanching noodles and for scooping ingredients out of any hot liquid.

Above: Draining spoons are useful for deep-frying and blanching.

COOKING TECHNIQUES

The traditional cooking methods of Malaysia require few culinary tools but a great deal of attention to detail. Fresh ingredients are of the utmost importance, followed by the balance of sharp or mild, salty or sweet, bitter or sour, or a combination of all of these flavours. The layering of ingredients is also important, especially in noodle dishes, where flavours and textures should complement each other but remain separate.

Many meals are prepared from scratch, starting with the plucking of chickens and grinding of spices, followed by grilling over charcoal, gentle simmering and steaming, or stir-frying. Armed with the correct equipment, the cooking is easy – most of the work, and the key to culinary success, is in the preparation.

STEAMING

This is a popular way of preparing delicate-tasting foods, such as fish and shellfish, pork-filled dumplings and sticky rice cakes wrapped in bamboo or banana leaves. Place the food in a bamboo steamer, which should be lined with leaves if the food isn't wrapped in them. Put the lid on the steamer and set it over a wok that is half-filled with water. Bring the water to the boil, then reduce the heat and steam the food according to the recipe.

Above: Fish wrapped in banana leaves with spices steams to perfumed perfection on a bamboo rack.

DRY-FRYING

Dried spices are often roasted before grinding to release their natural oils and enhance the aroma.

1 Spread the spices thinly in a wok or heavy pan and put it over a high heat.

2 As the pan begins to heat, shake it so that the spices don't get too brown.

3 Once the spices begin to colour and their aroma fills the air, put them in a mortar and grind to a powder.

BRAISING

The classic slow-cooking method is braising. Oily fish, duck and red meat are often cooked this way, with herbs, spices and coconut milk or juice.

Traditionally, to seal in the moisture, a covered clay pot is used. Placed over a medium heat, or in the oven, cooking can take from 30 minutes to 2 hours, depending on the dish. If you don't have a clay pot, use a heavy-based casserole. The key is in containing the moisture and even heat distribution, so don't use a thin aluminium pot. Simply put all the ingredients in a clay pot and place in a preheated oven. (It can also be placed over a medium heat on the stove if you prefer.)

GRILLING OVER CHARCOAL

As conventional grills (broilers) don't exist in most homes in Southeast Asia, grilling is generally done outdoors over hot charcoal.

This traditional method of cooking not only lends itself to many types of food, it also enhances the taste. Whole fish, pigs or chickens can be cooked this way. Tasty, marinated morsels of food, skewered on bamboo sticks and grilled in the streets, make popular snacks. When cooking over charcoal, light the coals and wait until they are covered with grey or white ashes. If the charcoal is too hot, the food will just burn.

Wooden and bamboo skewers
If you are using wooden or bamboo skewers, soak them in water for about 30 minutes before using to prevent them from burning.

STIR-FRYING

Of all the cooking techniques, this is the most important one in Malaysia. The technique is more in the preparation of ingredients than in the cooking process, which takes only minutes. Generally, the ingredients should be cut or shredded into bitesize morsels and laid out in the order in which they are to be cooked. To stir-fry successfully you need a wok, placed over a high heat, and a ladle or spatula to toss the ingredients around, so that they cook but still retain their freshness and crunchy texture.

In stir frying, the key is to work quickly and layer the ingredients according to the length of time they require for cooking. Serve the dish hot straight from the wok into warmed bowls and don't leave the food sitting in the wok – it must be enjoyed fresh.

1 Pour a little oil into the wok and place it over a high heat until hot.

2 Add the spices and aromatics to the oil – it should sizzle on contact – and toss them around to flavour the oil. It is important to keep stirring quickly in order to move the ingredients around the wok and ensure that they do not burn. They will release plenty of aroma.

3 Add the pieces of meat or fish, and toss them in the wok for two minutes.

4 Add the sliced firm vegetables or mushrooms and stir-fry for a minute.

5 Add the leafy vegetables or bean-sprouts and toss them around quickly.

6 Finally, toss in the herbs, seasonings or sauce, mix well and serve piping hot.

DEEP-FRYING

Use an oil that can be heated to a high temperature, such as groundnut (peanut) oil, and don't put in too much cold food at once, as this will cool the oil down.

1 Pour the oil into a wok or pan (filling it no more than two-thirds full) and heat to about 180°C/350°F. To test the temperature, add a drop of batter or a piece of onion. If it sinks, the oil is not hot enough; if it burns, it is too hot. If it sizzles and rises to the surface, the temperature is perfect.

2 Cook the food in small batches until crisp and lift out with a slotted spoon or wire mesh skimmer when cooked. Drain on a wire rack lined with kitchen paper and serve immediately, or keep warm in the oven until ready to serve.

BLANCHING

This method is often used to cook delicate meat such as chicken breast portions or duck.

Place the meat and any flavourings in a pan and add just enough water to cover. Bring to the boil, then remove from the heat and leave to stand, covered, for 10 minutes, then drain.

BROTHS AND SOUPY NOODLES

Steaming bowls of fragrant, clear broth brimming with noodles,

vegetables, succulent seafood and tender meat are the staple fare

of hawker stalls and coffee shops in Malaysia. Years ago,

itinerant hawkers used to roam the streets carrying a pole laden

with two baskets: one held a stove and a cooking pot, the other

held the ingredients for the soup, which could be quickly rustled

up for hungry customers.

NOODLES IN SPICY TANGY SOUP

THIS IS A CLASSIC NONYA DISH CALLED MEE SIAM, *WHICH HAS BEEN INFLUENCED BY THE FLAVOURINGS OF NEIGHBOURING THAILAND, WITH THE SOUR NOTES EMANATING FROM THE TAMARIND AND SALTED SOYA BEANS. ALMOST EVERY FOOD STALL IN MALAYSIA HAS ITS OWN VERSION OF* MEE SIAM, *WHICH IS ADAPTED TO SUIT MALAY, CHINESE OR INDIAN TASTES.*

SERVES FOUR

INGREDIENTS

vegetable oil, for deep-frying
225g/8oz firm tofu, rinsed, drained
    and cut into cubes
60ml/4 tbsp dried prawns (shrimp),
    soaked until rehydrated
5ml/1 tsp shrimp paste
4 garlic cloves, chopped
4–6 dried red chillies, soaked to
    soften, drained, seeded and the
    pulp scraped out
90g/3½oz/¾ cup roasted
    peanuts, ground
50g/2oz salted soya beans
2 lemon grass stalks, trimmed,
    halved and bruised
30ml/2 tbsp sugar
15–30ml/1–2 tbsp tamarind paste
150g/5oz dried rice vermicelli,
    soaked in hot water until pliable
a handful of beansprouts, rinsed
    and drained
4 quail's eggs, hard-boiled, shelled
    and halved
2 spring onions (scallions), sliced
salt and ground black pepper
fresh coriander (cilantro) leaves,
    finely chopped, to garnish

1 In a wok, heat enough vegetable oil for deep-frying. Drop in the tofu and deep-fry until golden. Drain on kitchen paper and set aside.

2 Using a mortar and pestle, grind the soaked dried prawns, shrimp paste, garlic and chilli pulp to a paste.

3 Heat 30ml/2 tbsp of oil in a wok and stir in the prawn, garlic and chilli paste. Fry for 1 minute until fragrant, then add the peanuts, salted soya beans and lemon grass.

4 Fry for another minute and stir in the sugar and tamarind paste, followed by 900ml/1½ pints/3¾ cups water. Mix well and bring to the boil. Reduce the heat and simmer for 10 minutes. Season with salt and pepper.

5 Drain the noodles and, using a sieve (strainer) or perforated ladle, plunge the noodles into the broth to heat through.

6 Divide the noodles among individual serving bowls, sprinkle over the beansprouts and add the deep-fried tofu, halved quail's eggs and sliced spring onions.

7 Ladle the spicy broth over the top, garnish with the coriander and serve immediately while hot.

COOK'S TIP

This is such a tasty, spicy dish that it is best served on its own as a light meal or nourishing snack so that the flavours can be fully appreciated.

Per Portion Energy 547Kcal/2280kJ; Protein 29.5g; Carbohydrate 42.5g, of which sugars 10g; Fat 29g, of which saturates 4.4g; Cholesterol 48mg; Calcium 389mg; Fibre 3.7g; Sodium 203mg.

PEPPERY VEGETABLE SOUP

OF INDONESIAN ORIGIN, THIS IS A SIMPLE VERSION OF A RICHER SPICED SOUP KNOWN AS SOTO.
IT CAN BE COOKED WITH WATER BUT USING A VEGETABLE STOCK, IDEALLY A HOME-MADE ONE, GIVES
THE DISH MUCH MORE BODY AND DEPTH OF FLAVOUR. IT SHARPENS THE TASTE BUDS WITHOUT BEING
TOO FILLING, AND IS IDEAL AS A STARTER IN A MEAL THAT FEATURES SPICY MEAT OR FISH DISHES.

SERVES FOUR

INGREDIENTS
- 100g/3¾oz carrots, peeled
- 100g/3¾oz cucumber
- 100g/3¾oz French (green) or long (snake) beans
- 5ml/1 tsp black peppercorns
- 2 shallots
- 2 garlic cloves
- 25g/1oz fresh root ginger
- 30ml/2 tbsp vegetable oil
- 700ml/24fl oz/2¾ cups water or vegetable stock
- salt
- fried shallots, to garnish

COOK'S TIP
Most supermarkets and ethnic stores now sell fried shallots in small tubs.

1 Peel the carrots and cut them into 1cm/½in cubes. Trim the beans and slice them into rounds of a size similar to the other vegetables.

2 Peel the cucumber and scoop the seeds out, then dice it.

3 Grind the peppercorns, shallots, garlic and ginger to a paste. Heat the oil and fry the paste for 3 minutes. Add the water or stock and bring to the boil.

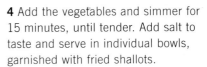

4 Add the vegetables and simmer for 15 minutes, until tender. Add salt to taste and serve in individual bowls, garnished with fried shallots.

Per portion Energy 72kcal/297KJ; Protein 1.1g; Carbohydrate 4.3g, of which sugars 3.6g; Fat 5.8g, of which saturates 0.7g; Cholesterol 0mg; Calcium 24mg; Fibre 1.5g; Sodium 117mg.

HOT AND SOUR FISH SOUP

IKAN ASAM PEDAS IS THE MALAY VERSION OF THE HOT AND SOUR FISH SOUP FOUND THROUGHOUT SOUTH-EAST ASIA. THE SOUR NOTES ARE DERIVED FROM THE USE OF TAMARIND, WHEREAS THE HOT FLAVOURINGS COME FROM THE CHILLI-BASED REMPAH. THE PERANAKANS SERVE THEIR VERSION OF THIS SOUP WITH STEAMED RICE, BUT MOST MALAYS EAT IT WITH CHUNKS OF BREAD.

SERVES FOUR

INGREDIENTS
    30ml/2 tbsp vegetable oil
    15–30ml/1–2 tbsp tamarind paste
    115g/4oz yard-long beans, cut into
      short lengths
    450g/1lb fish cutlets (such as trout,
      cod, sea perch, pike), about
      2.5cm/1in thick
    fresh coriander (cilantro) leaves,
      to garnish
    rice or bread, to serve
For the rempah
    8 dried red chillies, soaked in warm
      water until soft, drained and seeded
    8 shallots, chopped
    4 garlic cloves, chopped
    2 lemon grass stalks, sliced
    25g/1oz fresh galangal, chopped
    25g/1oz fresh turmeric, chopped
    5ml/1 tsp shrimp paste

1 To make the rempah, grind all the rempah ingredients to a paste, using a mortar and pestle or food processor.

2 Heat the oil in a wok or heavy pan, and stir in the rempah. Fry it until it is fragrant and begins to change colour. Stir in the tamarind paste and add the yard-long beans, tossing them around the wok until they are well coated in the spice mixture.

3 Pour in 900ml/1½ pints/3¾ cups water and bring to the boil. Reduce the heat and simmer for 5 minutes.

4 Season the broth to taste with salt and pepper, then add the fish cutlets. Cook gently for 2–3 minutes until cooked through, then ladle the soup into bowls. Garnish with coriander and serve with steamed rice or chunks of fresh bread.

Per Portion Energy 164Kcal/686kJ; Protein 21.7g; Carbohydrate 4.9g, of which sugars 3.5g; Fat 6.5g, of which saturates 0.8g; Cholesterol 52mg; Calcium 33mg; Fibre 1.3g; Sodium 69mg.

CHINESE FISH BALL SOUP

THIS LIGHT CHINESE SOUP CAN BE FOUND IN COFFEE SHOPS AND AT THE TZE CHAR STALLS, WHERE THE FOOD IS ORDERED FROM THE MENU AND COOKED ON THE SPOT. OFTEN EATEN AS A SNACK OR LIGHT LUNCH, THE SOUP IS GARNISHED WITH SPRING ONIONS AND FRESH CHILLIES, AND THE MALAYS OFTEN ADD AN EXTRA DRIZZLE OF CHILLI SAUCE OR A DOLLOP OF CHILLI SAMBAL.

SERVES FOUR TO SIX

INGREDIENTS

For the fish balls
    450g/1lb fresh fish fillets (such as haddock, cod, whiting or bream), boned and cubed
    15–30ml/1–2 tbsp rice flour
    salt and ground black pepper

For the soup
    1.5 litres/2½ pints/6¼ cups fish or chicken stock
    15–30ml/1–2 tbsp light soy sauce
    4–6 mustard green leaves, shredded
    90g/3½oz mung bean thread noodles, soaked in hot water until soft

For the garnish
    2 spring onions (scallions), trimmed and finely sliced
    1 red or green chilli, seeded and finely sliced
    fresh coriander (cilantro) leaves, finely chopped

COOK'S TIP
This soup is quite quick to make, but if you wish to do some of the preparation in advance the fish balls can be stored in the refrigerator for a few hours.

1 To make the fish balls, grind the flaked flesh to a paste, using a mortar and pestle or food processor. Season with salt and pepper and stir in about 60ml/4 tbsp water. Add enough rice flour to form a paste. Take small portions of fish paste into your hands and squeeze them to mould into balls.

2 Meanwhile, bring the stock to the boil in a deep pan and season to taste with soy sauce. Drop in the fish balls. Bring the stock back to the boil, then lower the heat and gently simmer for 5 minutes. Add the shredded mustard greens and cook with the fish balls for 1 minute until just tender.

3 Divide the noodles among four to six bowls. Using a slotted spoon, add the fish balls and greens, then ladle over the hot stock. Garnish with the spring onions and chilli and sprinkle the chopped coriander over the top.

Per Portion Energy 127Kcal/533kJ; Protein 14.9g; Carbohydrate 14.8g, of which sugars 0.5g; Fat 0.6g, of which saturates 0.1g; Cholesterol 35mg; Calcium 17mg; Fibre 0.2g; Sodium 408mg.

WON TON SOUP

POSSIBLY THE BEST-TRAVELLED CHINESE DISH OF ALL, WON TON SOUP IS NOW UBIQUITOUS IN RESTAURANTS, HAWKER CENTRES AND FOOD COURTS THROUGHOUT SOUTH-EAST ASIA. WON TONS ARRIVED WITH CANTONESE AND HAKKA MIGRANTS FROM SOUTH CHINA AND, IN TIME, WERE ADOPTED BY THE LOCALS. THIS SOUP IS ONE OF THE EASIEST AND TASTIEST STARTERS TO PREPARE AT HOME. ADDING A LITTLE CORNFLOUR TO THE FILLING GIVES IT A SMOOTH TEXTURE.

SERVES FOUR

INGREDIENTS

120g/4oz fresh prawns (shrimp), shelled
100g/3¾oz minced (ground) pork
5ml/1 tsp salt
5ml/1 tsp cornflour (cornstarch)
12 won ton wrappers
600 ml/1 pint/2½ cups water
1 seafood stock cube
1 spring onion (scallion), trimmed and chopped, to garnish
freshly ground black pepper

1 Grind the prawns finely using a pestle and mortar or a food processor and mix with the pork, salt and cornflour.

2 Lay a won ton wrapper flat on the work surface and moisten the edges with water. Place a scant teaspoonful of the mixture in the centre and gather up the sides around the filling to make a tight ball, pressing the wrapper firmly together at the neck to leave a little frill at the top. Repeat with the remaining mixture and won ton wrappers.

3 Bring a pot of water to the boil. Drop in the won tons and cook them for 3 minutes. Drain and set aside.

4 Bring the measured water to the boil, crumble in the stock cube and stir to dissolve. Drop the cooked won tons into the hot stock and cook for 1 minute.

5 Garnish with chopped spring onions and season with black pepper. Divide among four serving bowls and serve the soup immediately.

COOK'S TIP
Won ton wrappers are widely available in Chinese supermarkets.

Per portion Energy 134Kcal/568kJ; Protein 13.6g; Carbohydrate 16.3g, of which sugars 1.9g; Fat 2.1g, of which saturates 0.7g; Cholesterol 52mg; Calcium 42mg; Fibre 0.6g; Sodium 589mg.

EURASIAN CURRIED SOUP

WITH A CULINARY CULTURE BORN FROM INDIAN, MALAY, CHINESE AND EUROPEAN TRADITIONS, THE EURASIANS HAVE SOME DISTINCT DISHES OF THEIR OWN. BECAUSE THEY TRACE THEIR ROOTS TO MELAKA DURING THE DUTCH AND PORTUGUESE PERIODS, MANY OF THE DISHES ARE LINKED TO THAT REGION AND EMPLOY PORTUGUESE METHODS, SUCH AS COOKING IN EARTHENWARE POTS. CHICKEN FEET ARE SOMETIMES ADDED TO THE STOCK IN THIS RECIPE TO ENRICH IT.

SERVES FOUR TO SIX

INGREDIENTS
1 chicken, about 1kg/2¼lb
2 chicken feet (optional)
2 cinnamon sticks
5ml/1 tsp black peppercorns
5ml/1 tsp fennel seeds
5ml/1 tsp cumin seeds
15 ml/1 tbsp ghee or vegetable oil
  with a little butter
15–30ml/1–2 tbsp brown
  mustard seeds
a handful of fresh curry leaves
salt and ground black pepper
2 limes, quartered, to serve
For the curry paste
40g/1½oz fresh root ginger, peeled
  and chopped
4 garlic cloves, chopped
4 shallots, chopped
2 lemon grass stalks, trimmed and
  chopped
4 dried red chillies, soaked to soften,
  drained, seeded and the pulp
  scraped out
15–30ml/1–2 tbsp Indian curry
  powder
salt and ground black pepper

1 To make the curry paste, grind the ginger with the garlic, shallots and lemon grass, using a mortar and pestle or food processor. Add the chilli pulp and curry powder and set aside.

2 Put the chicken and the chicken feet, if using, in a deep pan with the cinnamon sticks, peppercorns, fennel and cumin seeds. Add enough water to just cover, and bring it to the boil. Reduce the heat and cook gently for about 1 hour, until the chicken is cooked through.

3 Using two forks, remove the chicken from the broth, skin it and shred the meat. Strain the broth through a sieve (strainer).

4 In an earthenware pot or wok, heat the ghee or oil. Stir in the mustard seeds and, once they begin to pop and give off a nutty aroma, add the curry paste. Fry the paste until fragrant, then pour in the strained broth. Bring the broth to the boil and season to taste with salt and pepper.

5 Add the curry leaves and shredded chicken, and ladle the soup into bowls. Serve with wedges of lime to squeeze into the soup.

Per Portion Energy 264Kcal/1093kJ; Protein 20.7g; Carbohydrate 1.6g, of which sugars 1g; Fat 19.4g, of which saturates 6.3g; Cholesterol 112mg; Calcium 19mg; Fibre 0.5g; Sodium 104mg.

Indian Mutton Soup

Sop kambing is a popular dish at the Muslim and Malay hawker stalls as well as in the coffee shops. It is a warming, substantial soup that comes into its own late at night, when it is valued for its restorative qualities. It also makes a great supper dish, served with chunks of crusty bread or Indian flatbread.

SERVES FOUR TO SIX

INGREDIENTS

  25g/1oz fresh root ginger, peeled
    and chopped
  4–6 garlic cloves, chopped
  1 red chilli, seeded and chopped
  15ml/1 tbsp ghee or vegetable oil
  5ml/1 tsp coriander seeds
  5ml/1 tsp cumin seeds
  5ml/1 tsp ground fenugreek
  5ml/1 tsp sugar
  450g/1lb meaty mutton ribs, cut into
    bitesize pieces
  2 litres/3½ pints/7¾ cups lamb stock
    or water
  10ml/2 tsp tomato purée (paste)
  1 cinnamon stick
  4–6 cardamom pods, bruised
  2 tomatoes, peeled and quartered
  salt and ground black pepper
  fresh coriander (cilantro) leaves,
    roughly chopped, to garnish

1 Using a mortar and pestle or a food processor, grind the ginger, garlic and chilli to a paste.

2 Heat the ghee or oil in a wok or heavy pan and stir in the coriander and cumin seeds. Add the ginger, garlic and chilli paste along with the fenugreek and sugar. Stir until the mixture is fragrant and beginning to colour. Add the chopped mutton ribs, searing the meat on both sides.

3 Pour in the stock or water and stir in the tomato purée, cinnamon stick and cardamom pods. Bring to the boil, then reduce the heat, cover the pan and simmer gently for 1½ hours, until the meat is very tender and starting to fall away from the bones.

4 Season to taste with salt and pepper. Stir in the tomatoes, and garnish with coriander. Serve hot with chunks of fresh crusty bread or Indian flatbread.

Per Portion Energy 166Kcal/693kJ; Protein 15.2g; Carbohydrate 2.8g, of which sugars 2.5g; Fat 10.6g, of which saturates 5.2g; Cholesterol 62mg; Calcium 12mg; Fibre 0.5g; Sodium 87mg.

INDIAN SPICY NOODLES

THERE ARE VERY FEW NOODLE DISHES IN INDIAN COOKING, BUT MEE REBUS IS ONE OF THE BETTER KNOWN. IT'S REALLY A HYBRID, AS IT USES CHINESE INGREDIENTS SUCH AS PRESERVED SOY BEANS AND WHEAT NOODLES, LIBERALLY SPICED WITH INDIAN AND MALAY SPICES. REBUS MEANS "BOILED" IN MALAY, AND THE DISH IS ESSENTIALLY BOILED NOODLES WITH A THICK, SWEET, SPICY SAUCE.

SERVES FOUR

INGREDIENTS
  400g/14oz fresh egg noodles
  150g/5oz beansprouts
For the gravy
  10 dried red chillies, soaked until
    soft, squeezed dry and seeded
  5 candlenuts
  115g/4oz onion, sliced
  15g/½oz galangal, peeled
    and chopped
  25g/1oz ground coriander
  75g/3oz preserved soy (yellow)
    beans, crushed
  800ml/28 fl oz/3½ cups water
  500g/1¼lb sweet potatoes, boiled
    and mashed
  45ml/3 tbsp vegetable oil
  1 beef stock cube
  5ml/1 tsp salt
For the garnishes
  4 hard-boiled eggs, quartered
  30ml/2 tbsp fried shallots
  5 green chillies, sliced
  4 limes
  30ml/2 tbsp dark soy sauce
  fresh celery leaves

1 To make the gravy, grind the chillies, candlenuts, onion and galangal to a smooth paste. Dry fry the ground coriander in a wok over a low heat for 2 minutes and mix into the paste.

2 Heat the oil in a wok or large pan and fry the mixture for 2 minutes, then stir in the soy beans. Add the water and crumble in the stock cube.

3 Bring the stock to the boil and add the mashed sweet potatoes. Season to taste with salt. Cook for 5 minutes, until the sauce is the consistency of thick cream. Remove from the heat and keep the sauce warm.

COOK'S TIP
Have some extra mashed sweet potato standing by if you like a thick sauce.

4 Bring a pan of water to the boil and blanch the beansprouts for 2 minutes. Drain. Do the same with the noodles. Divide the noodles and beansprouts among serving plates and pour a few spoonfuls of sauce over each portion.

5 Garnish each serving with eggs, shallots, green chillies, lime slices, dark soy sauce and fresh celery leaves.

Per portion Energy 615kcal/2598KJ; Protein 16.5g; Carbohydrate 105.4g, of which sugars 12.1g; Fat 17.3g, of which saturates 3.5g; Cholesterol 30mg; Calcium 87mg; Fibre 8g; Sodium 906mg.

FRIED AND GRILLED SNACKS

The appetizing snacks in this chapter are staples of the vibrant
street food scene in Malaysia. Often eaten hot and fresh from
the grill (broiler), they make ideal finger food — there are
savoury toasts, crispy seafood, and succulent bitesize morsels of
eggs, oysters and fish cooked in crisp batter, and tender pieces
of meat such as the classic chicken satay, threaded on sticks and
all ready to dip into a delicious spicy sauce.

FRIED HARD-BOILED EGGS IN HOT RED SAUCE

A POPULAR SNACK AT MALAY STALLS, THIS SPICY EGG DISH ORIGINALLY CAME FROM INDONESIA. SERVED WRAPPED IN A BANANA LEAF, THE MALAYS OFTEN EAT IT WITH PLAIN STEAMED RICE, SLICED CHILLIES, ONION AND CORIANDER – IDEAL FOR A QUICK, TASTY SNACK OR LIGHT LUNCH.

SERVES FOUR

INGREDIENTS
vegetable oil, for deep-frying
8 eggs, hard-boiled and shelled
1 lemon grass stalk, trimmed,
  quartered and crushed
2 large tomatoes, skinned, seeded
  and chopped to a pulp
5–10ml/1–2 tsp sugar
30ml/2 tbsp dark soy sauce
juice of 1 lime
fresh coriander (cilantro) and mint
  leaves, coarsely chopped, to garnish
For the rempah
  4–6 red chillies, seeded and chopped
  4 shallots, chopped
  2 garlic cloves, chopped
  2.5ml/½ tsp shrimp paste

1 Using a mortar and pestle or food processor, grind the ingredients for the rempah to form a smooth paste. Set aside.

2 Heat enough oil for deep-frying in a wok or heavy pan and deep-fry the whole boiled eggs until golden brown. Lift them out and drain.

3 Reserve 15ml/1 tbsp of the oil and discard the rest. Heat the oil in the wok or heavy pan and stir in the rempah until it becomes fragrant. Add the lemon grass, followed by the tomatoes and sugar. Cook for 2–3 minutes, until it forms a thick paste.

4 Reduce the heat and stir in the soy sauce and lime juice. Add 30ml/2 tbsp water to thin the sauce. Toss in the eggs, making sure they are thoroughly coated, and serve hot, garnished with chopped coriander and mint leaves.

COOK'S TIP
If you don't want to deep-fry the eggs, plain hard-boiled eggs can be heated up in the spicy sauce.

Per Portion Energy 271Kcal/1125kJ; Protein 13.3g; Carbohydrate 5.5g, of which sugars 5g; Fat 22.3g, of which saturates 4.4g; Cholesterol 381mg; Calcium 67mg; Fibre 0.7g; Sodium 679mg.

FRIED DRIED ANCHOVIES
WITH PEANUTS

THE MALAYS AND PERANAKANS LOVE FRIED DRIED ANCHOVIES, IKAN BILIS GORENG. GENERALLY, THEY ARE SERVED AS A SNACK WITH BREAD OR AS AN ACCOMPANIMENT TO NASI LEMAK (COCONUT RICE). THE MALAYS ALSO ENJOY THEM WITH BUBUR (RICE PORRIDGE), FOR BREAKFAST.

SERVES FOUR

INGREDIENTS

4 shallots, chopped
2 garlic cloves, chopped
4 dried red chillies, soaked in warm water until soft, then seeded and chopped
30ml/2 tbsp tamarind pulp, soaked in 150ml/¼ pint/⅔ cup water until soft
vegetable oil, for deep-frying
115g/4oz/1 cup peanuts
200g/7oz dried anchovies, heads removed, washed and drained
30ml/2 tbsp sugar
bread or rice, to serve

1 Using a mortar and pestle or food processor, grind the shallots, garlic and chillies to a coarse paste. Squeeze the tamarind pulp to help soften it in the water and press it through a sieve (strainer). Measure out 120ml/4fl oz/ ½ cup of the tamarind water.

2 Heat enough oil for deep-frying in a wok. Add the anchovies to the oil and deep-fry until brown and crisp. Drain the anchovies on kitchen paper.

3 Lower the heat and deep-fry the peanuts in a wire basket, until they colour. Drain them on kitchen paper.

4 Pour out most of the oil from the wok, reserving 30ml/2 tbsp. Stir in the spice paste and fry until fragrant. Add the sugar, anchovies and peanuts. Gradually stir in the tamarind water, allowing it to evaporate and be soaked in so that the mixture remains dry.

5 Serve the dish hot or cold with bread or blended with steamed rice.

Per Portion Energy 338Kcal/1400kJ; Protein 17g; Carbohydrate 4.8g, of which sugars 2.6g; Fat 28g, of which saturates 4.4g; Cholesterol 24mg; Calcium 134mg; Fibre 2g; Sodium 1475mg.

GRILLED TAMARIND PRAWNS

THE AROMA EMANATING FROM THE MALAY GRILL STALLS AS LARGE, MARINATED PRAWNS ARE GRILLED OVER CHARCOAL MAKES YOU FEEL VERY HUNGRY. RATHER EXPERTLY, THE MALAYSIANS CRUNCH THE WHOLE PRAWN, SUCKING IN ALL THE TAMARIND FLAVOURING WHILE SPITTING OUT THE BITS OF SHELL.

SERVES TWO TO FOUR

INGREDIENTS

    500g/1¼ lb fresh, large prawns
      (shrimp)
    45ml/3 tbsp tamarind pulp
    30ml/2 tbsp kecap manis
    15ml/1 tbsp sugar
    ground black pepper
    fresh coriander (cilantro) leaves and
      2–4 green chillies, seeded and
      quartered lengthways, to garnish

1 Devein the prawns and remove the feelers and legs. Rinse well, pat dry with kitchen paper and, using a sharp knife, make an incision along the curve of the tail.

2 Put the tamarind pulp in a bowl and add 250ml/8fl oz/1 cup warm water. Soak the pulp until soft, squeezing it with your fingers to help it dissolve in the water. Strain the liquid and discard any fibre.

3 In a bowl, mix together the strained tamarind juice with the kecap manis, sugar and black pepper.

4 Pour the mixture over the prawns, rubbing it over the shells and into the incisions in the tails. Cover the bowl and leave to marinate for 1 hour.

5 Prepare the charcoal, or heat a conventional grill (broiler) to a high heat, and place the prawns on the rack.

6 Grill (broil) the prawns for about 3 minutes on each side until they are cooked through, brushing them with the marinade as they cook.

7 Serve immediately, garnished with coriander and chillies.

VARIATION
The seasonings and method of cooking in this recipe works well with other shellfish, as well as with meat and poultry such as ribs, chicken wings and drumsticks. The dish makes a tangy addition to a barbecue – cook it on a clean griddle to keep the flavours pure.

Per Portion Energy 74Kcal/309kJ; Protein 11.4g; Carbohydrate 4.9g, of which sugars 4.8g; Fat 1.1g, of which saturates 0.3g; Cholesterol 39mg; Calcium 97mg; Fibre 0.6g; Sodium 1301mg.

PRAWN AND SESAME TOASTS

THESE IRRESISTIBLE LITTLE TOAST TRIANGLES ARE A POPULAR HOT SNACK PREPARED BY CHINESE COOKS, MAKING USE OF THE WHITE BREAD INTRODUCED TO SOUTH-EAST ASIA BY EUROPEAN SETTLERS. THEY ARE SURPRISINGLY EASY TO PREPARE AND YOU CAN COOK THEM IN A FEW MINUTES.

SERVES FOUR

INGREDIENTS

225g/8oz peeled raw prawns (shrimp)
15ml/1 tbsp sherry
15ml/1 tbsp soy sauce
30ml/2 tbsp cornflour (cornstarch)
2 egg whites, whisked until stiff
4 slices white bread
115g/4oz/½ cup sesame seeds
oil, for deep-frying
sweet chilli sauce, to serve

1 Process the prawns, sherry and soy sauce in a food processor. Add the whisked egg whites with the cornflour and lightly but thoroughly fold them together until well blended.

2 Cut each slice of bread into four triangular quarters. Spread out the sesame seeds on a large plate.

3 Spread the prawn paste over one side of each bread triangle, then press the coated sides into the sesame seeds so that they stick and cover the prawn paste.

COOK'S TIPS

• Always use a very clean, dry bowl and whisk to prepare egg whites, otherwise they will fail to stiffen.
• Prepare the toasts a few hours ahead and chill them until you are ready to fry and serve them.
• The spicy, sweet dipping sauce on page 89 goes very well with these prawn toasts, but you can buy bottles of sauce for convenience.

4 Heat the oil in a wok or deep-fryer, to 190°C/375°F or until a cube of bread, added to the oil, browns in about 45 seconds. Add the toasts, a few at a time, prawn side down, and deep-fry for 2–3 minutes, then turn and fry on the other side until golden.

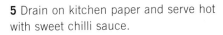

5 Drain on kitchen paper and serve hot with sweet chilli sauce.

Per portion Energy 433Kcal/1806kJ; Protein 19.1g; Carbohydrate 27.7g, of which sugars 1.2g; Fat 27.6g, of which saturates 3.6g; Cholesterol 110mg; Calcium 271mg; Fibre 2.7g; Sodium 559mg.

CRISPY PEPPERY SQUID

*THIS IS AN OFTEN-SEEN DISH AT SEAFOOD STALLS IN COASTAL TOWNS, WHERE SEAFOOD STALLS
PREDOMINATE. PEPPERY SQUID IS OFTEN SOLD TOGETHER WITH THE MUCH-LOVED DISH CHILLI
CRAB. CANTONESE CHEFS MAKE EXCELLENT USE OF FRESH BABY SQUID, WHICH ARE USUALLY COOKED
WHOLE IN THEIR INK. THEY ARE SO SMALL YOU CAN EAT THEM WHOLE.*

SERVES FOUR

INGREDIENTS
    24 small whole squid
    10ml/2 tsp cornflour (cornstarch)
    10ml/2 tsp freshly ground black
      pepper
    5ml/1 tsp salt
    oil for deep-frying
    sweet chilli sauce, to serve

COOK'S TIP
If baby squid are not available you can
use squid rings for this dish, although
the flavour will not be quite as good.

1 Wash the squid but leave them whole.
Dry them thoroughly and place them in
a plastic bag. Add the cornflour and
toss well to coat the squid.

2 Shake off the excess cornflour and
season the squid liberally with salt and
freshly ground pepper, pressing them
in firmly.

3 Heat the oil in a wok or heavy pan
and fry the squid until crispy, a few at a
time so that they do not stick together.

4 Reserve the fried squid on crumpled
paper on a warm plate until they are all
ready, and serve immediately with a
sweet chilli sauce and wedges of lemon
to squeeze over.

Per portion Energy 346kcal/1462kJ; Protein 31.2g; Carbohydrate 31.3g, of which sugars 2.6g; Fat 11.6g, of which saturates 1.8g; Cholesterol 422mg; Calcium 32mg; Fibre 0g; Sodium 1741mg.

DEEP-FRIED OYSTERS

EATING OYSTERS ON THE HALF SHELL IS NOT A COMMON MALAYSIAN PRACTICE AS THE LOCAL OYSTERS ARE NOT AS GOOD, BUT THEY DO LEND THEMSELVES TO COOKING IN INVENTIVE WAYS. THESE OYSTERS FRIED IN A LIGHT BATTER ARE CRISPY AND LIGHT AND SUCCULENT ON THE INSIDE.

SERVES FOUR

INGREDIENTS
16 large fresh oysters, shelled
oil for deep-frying
sweet chilli sauce or lime wedges,
   to serve

For the batter
50g/2oz rice flour
25g/1oz self-raising (self-rising) flour
100ml/3½ fl oz cold water
1 egg white

1 Wash and drain the oysters thoroughly. Blend the flours and stir in the cold water until well mixed.

2 Beat the egg white in a clean, dry bowl with an electric whisk until stiff peaks form, then fold it lightly into the batter. Stir thoroughly but gently until the batter is smooth.

3 Heat the oil in a wok or heavy pan. Dip each oyster in the batter and deep-fry for 1–2 minutes until brown and crispy. Serve with a sweet chilli sauce or a good squeeze of lime juice.

Per portion Energy 244kcal/1012kJ; Protein 6.4g; Carbohydrate 15.8g, of which sugars 0.1g; Fat 17.2g, of which saturates 2g; Cholesterol 23mg; Calcium 81mg; Fibre 0.5g; Sodium 242mg.

CHICKEN SATAY

THIS POPULAR DISH IS A DELICACY THAT EVERY SOUTH-EAST ASIAN COUNTRY CLAIMS AS THEIR OWN. HOWEVER, MALAYSIA CAN BOAST SOME OF THE BEST AVAILABLE, ESPECIALLY IN RURAL AREAS, AND IN SINGAPORE THE MANY SATAY STALLS ALONG BEACH ROAD IN THE 1950s CAME TO BE KNOWN AS THE SATAY CLUB. LEMON GRASS, BRUISED AT THE ROOT END, MAKES A FEATHERY BASTING BRUSH.

1 Blend together all the ingredients for the marinade in a non-metallic dish. Add the chicken and marinate for several hours or overnight.

2 To make the sauce, grind the onions, garlic, shrimp paste, galangal, lemon grass and chillies to make a fine paste. Heat the oil and fry the paste over medium heat for 15 minutes, stirring constantly. When the oil separates, add the tamarind blended with the water and bring to the boil. Season to taste with salt and sugar and simmer for 10 minutes.

3 Thread 3–4 pieces of chicken on to each stick, pressing them together. Grill (broil) over hot coals or under a hot grill (broiler) for 8 minutes, turning once.

4 Dip the lemon grass in oil and baste them to impart a delicious lemony tang.

5 Heat the sauce through, add the ground nuts and stir well. Remove from the heat immediately and serve with the satay sticks.

MAKES ABOUT 20–24 STICKS

INGREDIENTS
    500g/1¼lb chicken breast, cut into
        pieces 4 x 2.5 x 1cm/1½ x 1 x ½in
    20–24 bamboo or wooden skewers,
        soaked in water
For the marinade
    15ml/1 tbsp ground coriander
    15ml/1 tbsp ground cumin
    5ml/1 tsp ground turmeric
    5ml/1 tsp chilli powder
    150ml/5 fl oz/¾ cup coconut milk
    5ml/1 tsp salt
    10ml/2 tsp sugar
    45ml/3 tbsp oil
    1 stalk lemon grass, bruised at
        the root end to make a brush
For the sauce (makes about 1 litre/
1¾ pints/4 cups)
    2 large onions, roughly chopped

    4 cloves garlic, roughly chopped
    25g/1oz shrimp paste
    15g/½oz galangal, roughly chopped
    2 stalks lemon grass, 7.5cm/3in of
        root end
    10 dried chillies, soaked until soft
        and seeds removed (optional for
        milder flavour)
    300g/11oz peanuts, finely ground
    45ml/3 tbsp tamarind concentrate
    400ml/14 fl oz/1⅔ cups water
    10ml/2 tsp salt
    25g/1oz sugar
    150ml/5 fl oz/⅔ cup vegetable oil

COOK'S TIP
Add the ground peanuts to the sauce just before serving the satay, otherwise they tend to settle down and make the sauce too stiff. If this happens, warm it in a microwave oven for 1–2 minutes.

Per portion Energy 33Kcal/139kJ; Protein 7.1g; Carbohydrate 0.4g, of which sugars 0.3g; Fat 0.3g, of which saturates 0.1g; Cholesterol 20mg; Calcium 2mg; Fibre 0.1g; Sodium 107mg.

SPICY LENTIL AND MEAT PATTIES

OTHERWISE KNOWN AS SHAMI KEBABS, THESE DELIGHTFUL LENTIL AND LAMB PATTIES ARE POPULAR ON THE MARKET STALLS. ORIGINALLY OF INDIAN ORIGIN, THE SHAMI KEBABS OF MALAYSIA HAVE BEEN ADAPTED TO SUIT THE LOCAL TASTES, OFTEN SERVED WITH RICE AND A SAMBAL, OR EVEN BETWEEN CHUNKS OF BREAD WITH TOMATO KETCHUP, LIKE A BURGER.

SERVES FOUR

INGREDIENTS

150g/5oz/generous ½ cup red,
  brown, yellow or green lentils,
  rinsed
30ml/2 tbsp vegetable oil
2 onions, finely chopped
2 garlic cloves, finely chopped
1 green chilli, seeded and finely
  chopped
25g/1oz fresh root ginger,
  finely chopped
250g/9oz lean minced
  (ground) lamb
10ml/2 tsp Indian curry powder
5ml/1 tsp ground turmeric
4 eggs
vegetable oil, for shallow frying
salt and ground black pepper
fresh coriander (cilantro)
  leaves, roughly chopped,
  to garnish
1 lemon, quartered, to serve

COOK'S TIP
These patties are delicious served in a baguette, halved lengthways, layered with lettuce leaves, coriander (cilantro), mint, yogurt and a hot chutney or a chilli sauce.

1 Put the lentils in a pan and cover with plenty of cold water. Bring the water to the boil and cook gently until the lentils have softened but still have a little bite to them – this may take 20–40 minutes depending on the type of lentil you are using. Drain well.

2 Heat the oil in a heavy pan and stir in the onions, garlic, chilli and ginger. Fry until they begin to colour, then add the lentils and minced lamb. Cook for a few minutes, then add the curry powder and turmeric. Season with salt and pepper and cook the mixture over a high heat until the moisture has evaporated. The mixture needs to be dry for the patties.

3 Leave the meat mixture aside until it is cool enough to handle. Beat one of the eggs lightly and stir it into the meat.

4 Using your fingers, take small portions of the mixture and roll them into balls about the size of a plum or apricot. Press each ball in the palm of your hand to a form a thick, flat patty – if the mixture sticks to your hands, wet your palms with a little water.

5 Beat the remaining eggs in a bowl. Heat enough oil in a heavy pan for shallow frying. Dip each patty in turn in beaten egg and place them all in the hot oil. Fry for about 3–4 minutes each side, until golden. Garnish with fresh coriander and serve with lemon wedges to squeeze over.

Per Portion Energy 488Kcal/2033kJ; Protein 28g; Carbohydrate 25.7g, of which sugars 3.7g; Fat 31.2g, of which saturates 7.4g; Cholesterol 238mg; Calcium 87mg; Fibre 3.1g; Sodium 140mg.

RICE AND NOODLES

Either rice or noodles are eaten with every meal in Malaysia, from breakfast to late-night snacks, and many noodles are themselves made of rice. A bowl of simple steamed or boiled rice is filling and nourishing, and provides the background for vibrantly spiced meat, fish and vegetable accompaniments. Soft, comforting noodles are tossed into countless stir-fries to make satisfying and speedy meals.

MALAY YELLOW RICE

COLOURED A VIBRANT YELLOW WITH TURMERIC, NASI KUNING IS A DELICATELY FLAVOURED RICE DISH THAT IS OFTEN SERVED AT MALAY FESTIVALS. IT IS ALSO ONE OF THE POPULAR ITEMS AT MALAY NASI CAMPUR STALLS, WHERE IT IS SERVED WITH A VARIETY OF MEAT AND VEGETABLE DISHES. LONG GRAIN, SUCH AS JASMINE RICE, OR SHORT GRAIN OR STICKY RICE CAN BE USED FOR THIS DISH, WHICH IS COOKED IN THE SAME WAY AS PLAIN STEAMED RICE, USING THE ABSORPTION METHOD.

SERVES FOUR

INGREDIENTS

30ml/2 tbsp vegetable or sesame oil
3 shallots, finely chopped
2 garlic cloves, finely chopped
450g/1lb/generous 2 cups long grain
  rice, thoroughly washed and drained
400ml/14fl oz/1⅔ cups coconut milk
10ml/2 tsp ground turmeric
4 fresh curry leaves
2.5ml/½ tsp salt
ground black pepper
2 red chillies, seeded and finely
  sliced, to garnish

1 Heat the oil in a heavy pan and stir in the shallots and garlic. Just as they begin to colour, stir in the rice until it is coated in the oil.

2 Add 450ml/¾ pint/scant 2 cups water, the coconut milk, turmeric, curry leaves, salt and pepper. Bring to the boil, then turn down the heat and cover. Cook gently for 15–20 minutes, until all the liquid has been absorbed.

3 Turn off the heat and leave the rice to steam in the pan for 10 minutes. Fluff up the rice with a fork and serve garnished with red chillies.

COOK'S TIP
To serve neat individual portions of rice, pack it into ramekin dishes and unmould the rice on to each diner's plate.

Per Portion Energy 481Kcal/2011kJ; Protein 8.8g; Carbohydrate 95.9g, of which sugars 5.8g; Fat 6.4g, of which saturates 0.9g; Cholesterol 0mg; Calcium 54mg; Fibre 0.2g; Sodium 356mg.

GHEE RICE WITH TURMERIC

A COUSIN OF MALAY YELLOW RICE, THIS IS A MALAYSIAN/INDIAN VERSION THAT USES GHEE INSTEAD OF OIL. TRADITIONALLY SERVED WITH RICH LAMB CURRIES, IT IS OFTEN COOKED WITH GLUTINOUS RICE, WHOSE STARCHY TEXTURE MAKES IT EASIER TO SCOOP UP WHEN EATEN WITH THE FINGERS. BASMATI WILL DO AS WELL IF YOU USE A LITTLE MORE WATER THAN IS NEEDED WITH NORMAL RICE. THE ADDITION OF ROSE WATER GIVES IT A LOVELY PERFUME.

SERVES FOUR

INGREDIENTS

250g/9oz/1¼ cups basmati rice
400ml/14fl oz/1¾ cups water
10ml/2 tsp ground turmeric
30ml/2 tbsp ghee
15ml/1 tbsp rose water
red chillies, to garnish

1 Soak the rice in water for half an hour then place in a pan with the water, turmeric, ghee and rose water.

2 Bring the rice to the boil and simmer, tightly covered, for 10–15 minutes, until the water is absorbed. Remove from the heat and leave to steam, still covered, for 5–10 more minutes.

3 To make chilli flowers, cut four deep slits from tip to stalk, leaving the stalk end intact. Remove the seeds and soak the chillies in ice-cold water, where they will curl up. Wash your hands thoroughly after handling the chillies and be careful not to touch your eyes.

4 Transfer the rice to a bowl and turn it out to form a little mound. Serve on a banana leaf, garnished with the decorative chilli flowers.

Per portion Energy 299Kcal/1246kJ; Protein 5g; Carbohydrate 50.8g, of which sugars 0g; Fat 8.1g, of which saturates 3.6g; Cholesterol 0mg; Calcium 17mg; Fibre 0g; Sodium 1mg.

FRAGRANT COCONUT RICE

*NASI LEMAK, FRAGRANT COCONUT RICE, IS OFTEN FAVOURED BY MALAYS AND PERANAKANS.
THE MALAYS ARE PARTICULARLY FOND OF EATING NASI LEMAK WITH SAMBAL IKAN BILIS,
A SAUCE MADE WITH DRIED ANCHOVIES, CHILLIES AND SPICES, WHEREAS THE PERANAKANS
TEND TO TOP THEIRS WITH SAMBAL BELACAN, THE CHILLI AND SHRIMP PASTE.*

SERVES FOUR

INGREDIENTS

1 litre/1¾ pints/4 cups coconut
    milk
450g/1lb/2¼ cups short grain
    rice, thoroughly washed and
    drained
1 pandan (screwpine) leaf, tied
    in a loose knot
salt

1 Heat the coconut milk in a heavy pan and stir in the rice with a little salt. Add the knotted pandan leaf and bring the liquid to the boil.

2 Once the liquid is boiling, reduce the heat and simmer until the liquid has been absorbed by the rice.

3 Turn off the heat. Remove the lid and cover the pan with a clean dish towel, then replace the lid to keep the towel in place. Leave to steam for a further 15–20 minutes, then remove the pandan leaf and fluff up the rice with a fork before serving.

Per Portion Energy 459Kcal/1927kJ; Protein 9.1g; Carbohydrate 102g, of which sugars 12.3g; Fat 1.3g, of which saturates 0.5g; Cholesterol 0mg; Calcium 94mg; Fibre 0g; Sodium 275mg.

BUBUR

ORIGINATING FROM CHINA, THIS THICK RICE PORRIDGE OR CONGEE HAS BECOME POPULAR ALL OVER SOUTH-EAST ASIA. BUBUR IS THE MALAY NAME OF THE DISH. IT IS DESIGNED TO BE NOURISHING AND BLAND, AND THE MAIN INTEREST OF THE MEAL IS DERIVED FROM THE ADDITIONAL INGREDIENTS, OR OTHER DISHES, THAT ARE EATEN ALONGSIDE THE BUBUR.

SERVES FOUR TO SIX

INGREDIENTS

25g/1oz fresh root ginger, peeled and sliced
1 cinnamon stick
2 star anise
2.5ml/½ tsp salt
115g/4oz/½ cup short grain rice, thoroughly washed and drained

1 Bring 1.2 litres/2 pints/5 cups water to the boil in a heavy pan. Stir in the spices, the salt and the rice.

2 Reduce the heat, cover the pan, and simmer gently for 1 hour, or longer if you prefer a smoother, thicker and more porridge-like consistency.

3 Serve steaming hot as an accompaniment to highly flavoured or spicy meat, fish or vegetable dishes. You may prefer to remove the woody cinnamon sticks and star anise as they are inedible, but they make an attractive presentation.

COOK'S TIP
The Teochew version of bubur is called muay. With its addition of pickles and strips of omelette, it is popular for supper in Singapore. Bubur is enjoyed by Malays for breakfast with fried or grilled fish, chicken and beef, as well as pickles. Often flavoured with ginger, cinnamon and star anise, bubur is usually cooked until it is thick but the grains are still visible, whereas some of the Chinese versions are cooked for longer so that the rice breaks down completely. The consistency varies from family to family.

Per Portion Energy 69Kcal/288kJ; Protein 1.4g; Carbohydrate 15.3g, of which sugars 0g; Fat 0.1g, of which saturates 0g; Cholesterol 0mg; Calcium 4mg; Fibre 0g; Sodium 164mg.

MUSHROOM CLAY POT RICE

CLAY POTS ARE OFTEN REFERRED TO IN THE CANTONESE DIALECT AS "SAND POTS" OR SAR PO. THESE ARE VERY HANDY AS, IF PROPERLY SEASONED, THEY CAN GO STRAIGHT FROM THE FIRE TO THE TABLE, WHICH MAKES LIFE EASY AND LOOKS GOOD. HOWEVER, IF YOU ARE WORRIED THAT YOUR POT MAY CRACK OVER DIRECT HEAT, A SAFER METHOD IS TO COOK THE RICE IN A WOK OR PAN AND TRANSFER IT TO AN OVEN-WARMED CLAY POT TO SERVE.

SERVES FOUR

INGREDIENTS
    250g/9oz/1¼ cups jasmine rice
    400ml/14fl oz/1⅔ cups water
    30ml/2 tbsp vegetable oil
    15ml/1 tbsp sesame oil
    8 dried Chinese black (shiitake)
      mushrooms, soaked until soft, or
      8 canned mushrooms
    3 garlic cloves, crushed
    30g/2 tbsp oyster sauce
    5ml/1 tsp freshly ground black
      pepper

1 Place the rice in a pan with the water, bring to the boil and simmer, tightly covered, for about 20 minutes, until the water is absorbed. Remove from the heat and leave to steam for 10 minutes. Alternatively, cook the rice in the normal way in a microwave or rice cooker.

2 While the rice is cooking, prepare the topping. Slice the Chinese mushrooms into strips. Heat the oil in a wok or pan and fry the garlic until golden brown. Add the sliced mushrooms and stir-fry for 2 minutes.

3 Add the oyster sauce and the black pepper. Pour in 100ml/3½fl oz/scant ½ cup water and continue to stir for 2 minutes.

4 Pre-heat a clay pot in a hot oven for 10 minutes.

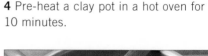

5 About 5 minutes before the rice is done, pile the mushrooms on top and cover the pan to finish cooking.

6 Remove the warmed claypot from the oven and transfer the rice and mushroom mixture to it to serve.

Per portion Energy 315Kcal/1312kJ; Protein 5.3g; Carbohydrate 53.2g, of which sugars 3.2g; Fat 8.7g, of which saturates 1.1g; Cholesterol 0mg; Calcium 15mg; Fibre 0.4g; Sodium 185mg.

FISH CONGEE

WHAT THE WESTERN WORLD KNOWS AS CONGEE, TO THE CHINESE IS SUSTENANCE, COMING AS IT DID FROM THE KITCHENS OF HUMBLE FAMILIES WHO HAD TO EKE OUT THEIR RATION OF RICE DURING LEAN MONTHS. TODAY, THIS PEASANT DISH HAS BEEN ELEVATED TO FIVE-STAR RESTAURANT STATUS BUT IT STILL RETAINS ITS HUMBLE CHARACTER. IT WAS TRADITIONALLY COOKED WITH BROKEN RICE, BUT JASMINE RICE, WHEN COOKED FOR A LONG PERIOD, HAS THE RIGHT PORRIDGE-LIKE CONSISTENCY.

SERVES FOUR

INGREDIENTS
- 115g/4oz jasmine rice
- 1 litre/1¾ pints/4 cups water
- 200g/7oz fillets of meaty fish such as snapper, grouper or cod
- 30ml/2 tbsp light soy sauce
- 1 fish stock (bouillon) cube
- 30ml/2 tbsp sesame oil

For the garnish
- 15ml/1 tbsp preserved winter vegetable (dung choy)
- 25g/1oz fresh root ginger, finely shredded
- 2 spring onions (scallions), chopped

1 Put the rice in a pan with the water. Bring to the boil and simmer for 1 hour. You may have to add more hot water if the congee becomes too thick.

2 Slice the fish into small pieces and add in the last 10 minutes, with the soy sauce, stock cube and sesame oil. Cook for 5 minutes and serve hot in individual bowls with the garnishes.

Per portion Energy 330Kcal/1384kJ; Protein 10.9g; Carbohydrate 56.2g, of which sugars 2.8g; Fat 7g, of which saturates 0.8g; Cholesterol 0mg; Calcium 56mg; Fibre 2.1g; Sodium 64mg.

LENTILS WITH GINGER AND COCONUT MILK

Though not a rice or noodle dish, dhal (meaning either lentils or the cooked dish) is so popular — either eaten simply with rice or Indian bread, or as part of a more elaborate meal — that it could not be left out. For the largely vegetarian South Indian immigrants who introduced it, dhal is an important source of protein. It makes a fabulous vegetarian addition to a Malaysian feast, or a simple and satisfying dish for an everyday supper.

1 Heat the ghee, or the oil and butter, in a heavy pan. Stir in the onion, garlic, chillies and ginger and fry until they are fragrant and beginning to colour. Add the sugar, cumin seeds, turmeric and garam masala, taking care not to burn the spices.

2 Stir in the lentils and coat in the spices and ghee. Pour in 600ml/ 1 pint/2½ cups water, mix thoroughly, and bring to the boil. Reduce the heat to a gentle simmer for 35–40 minutes until the mixture is thick.

3 Stir in the coconut milk and continue to simmer for a further 30 minutes until thick and mushy – if at any time the dhal seems too dry, add more water or coconut milk. Season to taste with salt.

4 In a small pan, heat the mustard seeds. As soon as they begin to pop, add the curry leaves and chillies. When the chillies begin to darken, stir in the ghee until it melts.

5 Spoon the mixture over the dhal, or fold it in until well mixed. Serve the dhal with yogurt or as part of an Indian-style meal, with curry, rice and chutney.

COOK'S TIP
Ghee is made by simmering unsalted butter until the liquid has evaporated and the solids settle at the bottom of the pan. The clarified oil is then skimmed off. It is usually sold in jars.

SERVES FOUR

INGREDIENTS
- 30ml/2 tbsp ghee, or 15ml/1 tbsp vegetable oil and 15g/½oz/1 tbsp butter
- 1 onion, chopped
- 4 garlic cloves, chopped
- 2 red chillies, seeded and chopped
- 50g/2oz fresh root ginger, peeled and chopped
- 10ml/2 tsp sugar
- 7.5ml/1½ tsp cumin seeds
- 5ml/1 tsp ground turmeric
- 15ml/1 tbsp garam masala
- 225g/8oz/generous 1 cup brown lentils, washed thoroughly and drained
- 600ml/1 pint/2½ cups coconut milk
- salt
- yogurt or curry, rice and chutney, to serve

For the garnish
- 10ml/2 tsp mustard seeds
- a small handful dried curry leaves
- 1–2 dried red chillies
- 15ml/1 tbsp ghee

Per Portion Energy 322Kcal/1358kJ; Protein 14g; Carbohydrate 41.3g, of which sugars 10.6g; Fat 12.4g, of which saturates 5.7g; Cholesterol 0mg; Calcium 77mg; Fibre 3g; Sodium 186mg.

SPICY FRIED NOODLES

BOTH INDIAN AND MALAY HAWKERS OFTEN SELL MEE GORENG *TOGETHER WITH* MEE REBUS *BUT ITS INVENTION IS GENERALLY ATTRIBUTED TO THE CULINARY INGENUITY OF THE EARLY INDIAN MIGRANTS. IN MOST MALAYSIAN TOWNS YOU WILL FIND IT SOLD IN ESTABLISHMENTS KNOWN AS* MAMAK *SHOPS, A TERM THAT REFERS TO SOUTH INDIANS. THERE IS NO OTHER NOODLE DISH IN THE INDIAN CULINARY TRADITION, AND THIS VERSION IS PECULIAR TO MALAYSIA AND SINGAPORE.*

SERVES FOUR

INGREDIENTS
90ml/6 tbsp vegetable oil
15–30ml/1–2 tbsp tamarind
   concentrate
45ml/3 tbsp water
2 eggs
450g/1lb fresh yellow noodles
100g/3¾oz beansprouts
2 tomatoes, peeled and quartered
salt
lime or lemon wedges, to serve
For the spice paste
4 dried chillies
½ large onion
3 garlic cloves

COOK'S TIP
As a time-saving substitute for the spice paste, you can use a bottled chilli and garlic sauce in this recipe.

1 Grind the spice paste ingredients in a mortar and pestle or food processor until fine. Heat 60ml/4 tbsp oil in a wok and fry the paste over low heat for about 8 minutes, then add the tamarind concentrate and water. Stir for 2 minutes and remove from the heat.

2 Heat the remaining oil in a wok and fry the eggs until set. Cut up roughly and add the noodles and beansprouts.

3 Mix the eggs and vegetables vigorously, then add 30ml/2 tbsp of the spice paste. Stir fry for 1 minute.

4 Add the tomatoes and continue to cook, stirring constantly, until the tomatoes are soft and everything is well mixed. Season to taste with salt.

5 Serve immediately with a squeeze of lime or lemon juice.

Per portion Energy 421kcal/1771kJ; Protein 13.7g; Carbohydrate 58.9g, of which sugars 4.2g; Fat 16.2g, of which saturates 3.2g; Cholesterol 85mg; Calcium 165mg; Fibre 2.7g; Sodium 416mg.

MIXED SEAFOOD HOR FUN

HOR FUN IS THE CANTONESE NAME FOR STIR-FRIED RICE NOODLES, A POPULAR HAWKER STAPLE AS WELL AS A RESTAURANT DISH. IN MALAYSIA, IN THE TOWN OF IPOH ESPECIALLY, FRESH RICE NOODLES ARE REPUTED TO BE MADE TO A SECRET RECIPE THAT HAS FOUND LEGIONS OF FANS. AS A RESULT, IPOH HOR FUN HAS COME TO MEAN THE SUPERLATIVE VERSION OF THIS DISH.

SERVES FOUR

INGREDIENTS
150g/5oz rice sticks
8 raw tiger prawns (jumbo shrimp)
30ml/2 tbsp vegetable oil
½ large onion, sliced
100g/3¾oz squid rings
100g/3¾oz beansprouts
30ml/2 tbsp oyster sauce
2.5ml/½ tsp black pepper
150ml/¼ pint/⅔ cup water or
  fish stock
fresh or pickled chillies, to serve

COOK'S TIP
Rice sticks, or dried rice noodles, double in bulk when reconstituted. They are available in various thicknesses.

1 Bring a pan of water to the boil and cook the rice sticks according to the packet instructions or until soft. Taste a strand to check. Drain and set aside.

2 Shell and de-vein the prawns by making a deep slit down the back. This will also make them curl up nicely.

3 Heat the oil and fry the onion until soft. Add the prawns and squid and stir-fry for 2 minutes. Add the beansprouts, noodles, oyster sauce and pepper and stir to toss well. Add the water or stock and let it bubble and reduce. As soon as the sauce is thick, serve the noodles with sliced or pickled chillies.

Per portion Energy 259Kcal/1084kJ; Protein 15.3g; Carbohydrate 34g, of which sugars 2.6g; Fat 6.4g, of which saturates 0.8g; Cholesterol 154mg; Calcium 53mg; Fibre 0.5g; Sodium 251mg.

MALAY BEE HOON

IN MALAYSIA THERE ARE ENDLESS STIR-FRIED NOODLE DISHES. SOME OF THESE STILL FOLLOW CLASSIC CHINESE RECIPES; OTHERS HAVE BEEN INFLUENCED BY THE CHINESE BUT ADAPTED TO SUIT THE TASTES OF THE DIFFERENT COMMUNITIES. BEE HOON IS THE MALAY NAME FOR THE RICE VERMICELLI WHICH, IN THIS POPULAR SNACK, IS STIR-FRIED WITH PRAWNS AND LOTS OF CHILLI.

SERVES FOUR

INGREDIENTS

  30ml/2 tbsp vegetable oil
  1 carrot, cut into matchsticks
  225g/8oz fresh prawns
    (shrimp), peeled
  120ml/4fl oz/½ cup chicken stock
    or water
  30ml/2 tbsp light soy sauce
  15ml/1 tbsp dark soy sauce
  175g/6oz beansprouts
  115g/4oz mustard greens or pak choi
    (bok choy), shredded
  225g/8oz dried rice vermicelli,
    soaked in lukewarm water until
    pliable, and drained
  1–2 fresh red chillies, seeded and
    finely sliced, and fresh coriander
    (cilantro) leaves, roughly chopped,
    to garnish

For the rempah
  4 dried red chillies, soaked until
    soft and seeded
  4 garlic cloves, chopped
  4 shallots, chopped
  25g/1oz fresh root ginger, peeled
    and chopped
  5ml/1 tsp ground turmeric

1 Using a mortar and pestle or a food processor, grind the ingredients for the rempah to a paste.

2 Heat the oil in a wok or heavy pan, and stir in the rempah until it begins to colour and become fragrant.

3 Toss in the carrots for a minute, followed by the prawns. Pour in the stock or water and soy sauces and cook for 1 minute.

4 Add the beansprouts and the shredded mustard greens or pak choi, followed by the rice vermicelli. Toss well to make sure the vegetables and noodles are all well coated and heated through.

5 Transfer the noodles to a serving plate and garnish with sliced chillies and chopped coriander. Serve immediately.

Per Portion Energy 330Kcal/1377kJ; Protein 17.5g; Carbohydrate 49.9g, of which sugars 4.5g; Fat 6.6g, of which saturates 0.8g; Cholesterol 110mg; Calcium 125mg; Fibre 1.9g; Sodium 960mg.

FISH AND SHELLFISH

Seafood is one of the greatest glories of the cuisines of

Malaysia, as a huge variety of tropical fish and shellfish are

hauled from the seas and rivers every day, and sold in the wet

markets set up in every town and village. A myriad inventive

dishes range from elegantly steamed whole fish, scented with

ginger and other aromatics in the Chinese style, to a

chilli-infused Malay Fish Curry.

SPICED FISH CAKES

THE OILY FLESH OF MACKEREL IS GENERALLY USED FOR THIS NONYA DISH, IKAN OTAK OTAK. BAKED, STEAMED OR GRILLED OVER CHARCOAL, THEY CAN BE EATEN HOT OR COLD AS FISH CAKES, OR USED AS LITTLE PACKAGES OF FISH PASTE TO SPREAD ON TOAST OR COCKTAIL CANAPÉS. BANANA LEAVES ARE SOLD IN ASIAN MARKETS, BUT YOU COULD USE PREPARED VINE LEAVES OR ALUMINIUM FOIL.

2 Put the mackerel and lime leaves in a bowl. Pour in the spiced coconut cream and the beaten eggs. Season with salt and pepper.

3 Using a fork or your hand, gently toss the fish in the coconut cream and eggs until the fish is well coated.

4 Using a spoon, place 30ml/2 tbsp of the fish mixture just off centre on a square of banana leaf and fold the sides of the leaf over the top, leaving a little room for expansion.

5 Secure the package with a cocktail stick threaded through each end, and repeat with the rest of the mixture.

6 Preheat the oven to 200°C/400°F/Gas 6 or prepare a charcoal grill. Bake the fish cakes in the oven for 30 minutes, or grill them for 15 minutes each side.

7 Serve the fish cakes in the banana leaves for everyone to unwrap, with lime quarters for squeezing over and chilli or peanut sambal for dipping.

SERVES FOUR TO SIX

INGREDIENTS
    4 shallots, chopped
    1 lemon grass stalk, trimmed
      and chopped
    25g/1oz galangal, chopped
    4 candlenuts or macadamia
      nuts, roasted
    4 dried red chillies,
      soaked in warm water
      until soft, squeezed dry
      and seeded
    5ml/1 tsp shrimp paste
    5–10ml/1–2 tsp ground turmeric
    250ml/8fl oz/1 cup coconut cream
    15ml/1 tbsp dark soy sauce
    10ml/2 tsp palm sugar (jaggery)

    450g/1lb fresh mackerel, cleaned,
      skinned and flaked
    4–6 lime leaves, finely shredded
    2 eggs, lightly beaten
    salt and ground black pepper
    12 banana leaves, cut into pieces
      about 20cm/8in square
    cocktail sticks (toothpicks)
    2 limes, quartered lengthways, and
      chilli or peanut sambal, to serve

1 Using a mortar and pestle or food processor, grind the shallots, lemon grass, galangal, candlenuts or macadamia nuts and chillies to a paste. Beat in the shrimp paste and turmeric. Stir in the coconut cream, soy sauce and sugar until blended.

Per Portion Energy 396Kcal/1642kJ; Protein 19.5g; Carbohydrate 4.5g, of which sugars 4.2g; Fat 33.5g, of which saturates 16.1g; Cholesterol 117mg; Calcium 60mg; Fibre 0.5g; Sodium 382mg.

NEW YEAR RAW FISH SALAD

TO CELEBRATE THE LUNAR NEW YEAR, CHINESE FAMILIES IN MALAYSIA GET TOGETHER TO EAT SPECIAL DISHES SUCH AS THIS SALAD, YU SHENG, WHICH ALL THE DINERS MUST HELP TO MIX WITH THEIR CHOPSTICKS, WHILE THEY SHOUT "LO HEI" ("TOSS THE FISH") FOR GOOD LUCK. MANY CHINESE RESTAURANTS OFFER THIS FESTIVE DISH WITH THE ADDITION OF SLICED JELLYFISH.

SERVES FOUR TO SIX

INGREDIENTS

- 175g/6oz fresh tuna or salmon, finely sliced
- 115g/4oz white fish fillet, finely sliced
- 25g/1oz fresh root ginger, peeled and finely chopped
- 2 garlic cloves, crushed
- juice of 2 limes
- 225g/8oz mooli (daikon), cut into julienne strips
- 2 carrots, cut into julienne strips
- 1 small cucumber, peeled, seeded and cut into julienne strips
- 4 spring onions (scallions), trimmed and cut into julienne strips
- 1 pomelo, segmented and sliced
- 4 fresh kaffir lime leaves, cut into fine ribbons
- 50g/2oz preserved sweet melon, finely sliced
- 50g/2oz preserved sweet red ginger, finely sliced
- ground black pepper
- 30ml/2 tbsp roasted peanuts, coarsely crushed, to garnish

For the dressing
- 30ml/2 tbsp sesame oil
- 15ml/1 tbsp light soy sauce
- 15ml/1 tbsp red vinegar
- 30ml/2 tbsp sour plum sauce
- 2 garlic cloves, crushed
- 10ml/2 tsp caster (superfine) sugar

COOK'S TIP

The Chinese add jellyfish to this salad for the texture rather than the taste. If you would like to add a different ingredient for its texture, you could try 50g/2oz cubes of steamed or stir-fried firm tofu.

1 In a shallow, non-metallic, dish, toss the slices of fish with the ginger, garlic and lime juice. Season with black pepper and set aside for at least 30 minutes to marinate.

2 Place the mooli, carrots, cucumber, spring onions, pomelo and lime leaves in a large bowl. Add the pieces of preserved melon and ginger. Toss well for an even distribution of ingredients.

3 Mix together the ingredients for the dressing, adjusting the sweet and sour balance to taste.

4 Just before serving, place the marinated fish on top of the vegetables in the bowl. Pour the dressing over the top and sprinkle with the roasted peanuts. Place the bowl in the middle of the table and get everyone to toss the salad with their chopsticks.

Per Portion Energy 126Kcal/528kJ; Protein 13.2g; Carbohydrate 6.5g, of which sugars 6.4g; Fat 5.4g, of which saturates 1g; Cholesterol 22mg; Calcium 36mg; Fibre 1.3g; Sodium 222mg.

GRILLED MACKEREL WITH SOY SAUCE, CHILLI AND LIME SAMBAL

MACKEREL, WHEN IT IS REALLY FRESH, IS ABSOLUTELY DELICIOUS GRILLED AND EATEN WITH A SHARP CHILLI DIP. WHEN CHOOSING MACKEREL, LOOK FOR CLEAR, SILVERY SKIN AND BRIGHT EYES. WHEN YOU PRESS DOWN ON THE FLESH, IT SHOULD BE FIRM AND SPRING BACK A LITTLE. IF IT'S SOFT TO THE TOUCH, THE MACKEREL IS NOT FRESH ENOUGH AND NOT WORTH BUYING.

SERVES FOUR

INGREDIENTS
    2 whole mackerel, gutted and
      cleaned
    5ml/1 tsp salt
    15ml/1 tbsp light fish sauce
    15ml/1 tbsp lime juice
    30ml/2 tbsp vegetable oil
For the chilli and lime sambal
    2–3 red chillies, seeded and chopped
    juice of 2 limes
    5ml/1 tsp salt
    pinch of sugar

1 Preheat the grill (broiler) to high. Grind the chillies for the sambal and stir in the other ingredients. Set aside.

2 Rub the fish inside and outside with salt. Place on a sheet of aluminium foil on a rack over a roasting pan.

3 Brush with fish sauce, lime juice and oil and grill for 10–15 minutes, turning once. Serve with the sambal.

Per portion Energy 216kcal/895kJ; Protein 14.1g; Carbohydrate 0.3g, of which sugars 0.3g; Fat 17.6g, of which saturates 3.1g; Cholesterol 41mg; Calcium 9mg; Fibre 0g; Sodium 788mg.

STEAMED WHOLE FISH NONYA-STYLE

IN MALAY AND INDIAN COOKING, WHOLE FISH IS OFTEN GRILLED OR FRIED, WHEREAS THE CHINESE AND PERANAKANS PREFER TO STEAM IT. PLUMP POMFRET RANKS AS ONE OF THE FAVOURITES TO STEAM WHOLE, OFTEN WITH SUBTLE FLAVOURINGS SO AS NOT TO SPOIL THE FRESH TASTE OF THE FISH. THIS NONYA DISH IS PARTICULARLY POPULAR IN PENANG AND MELAKA.

SERVES FOUR

INGREDIENTS

  3 spring onions (scallions), trimmed
    into 2.5cm/1in pieces and cut
    into strips
  25g/1oz fresh root ginger, peeled
    and cut into 2.5cm/1in strips
  4 dried shiitake mushrooms, soaked in
    hot water until soft and squeezed dry
  1 whole fresh fish, such as pomfret
    (porgy) or sea bass, weighing about
    900g/2lb, gutted and cleaned
  30ml/2 tbsp vegetable or sesame oil
  30ml/2 tbsp light soy sauce
  salt and ground black pepper
  1 red chilli, seeded and cut into thin
    strips and fresh coriander (cilantro)
    leaves, to garnish
  steamed rice and chilli
    sambal, to serve

2 Fill a wok one-third of the way up with water. Place a metal steaming rack in the wok, cover with a lid and put the wok over the heat. Score the fish diagonally three or four times on each side and season with salt and pepper. Place it on a heatproof plate and scatter the spring onion, ginger and shitake mushrooms over it. Place the plate on the rack, cover and steam the fish for 15–20 minutes, until cooked.

COOK'S TIP
To check that the fish is done insert the point of a kitchen knife into the thickest part of the flesh: it should be just opaque and lift away from the bone.

3 When the fish is cooked, heat the oil in a small pan. Stir in the soy sauce and pour it over the fish. Garnish the dish with the chillies and coriander leaves and serve with steamed rice and chilli sambal.

1 Put the spring onions and ginger in a bowl. Trim the shiitake mushrooms, discarding the hard stems, and cut them into thin strips. Add them to the spring onions and ginger and mix well.

Per Portion Energy 278Kcal/1165kJ; Protein 43.7g; Carbohydrate 0.5g, of which sugars 0.5g; Fat 11.2g, of which saturates 1.6g; Cholesterol 180mg; Calcium 296mg; Fibre 0.1g; Sodium 423mg.

SPICED LOBSTER IN BANANA LEAF

ANY FOOD THAT IS SPICED AND WRAPPED IN BANANA LEAF BEFORE BEING GRILLED OR STEAMED IS GENERALLY CALLED OTAK OTAK IN MALAYSIA. OTAK OTAK IS OFTEN MADE WITH FISH, ESPECIALLY ON THE HAWKER STALLS IN COASTAL AREAS. THIS VERSION OF THE RECIPE USES LOBSTER FOR A SPECTACULAR PARTY PIECE, BUT YOU COULD USE THE SAME METHOD TO COOK ANY FIRM FISH.

SERVES FOUR

INGREDIENTS
  2 lobster tails, shelled and minced (ground) coarsely
  4 lime leaves, cut into fine ribbons
  5ml/1 tsp salt
  5ml/1 tsp sugar
  2 eggs, lightly beaten
  30ml/2 tbsp vegetable oil
  175ml/6fl oz/¾ cup coconut cream
  8 pieces banana leaf, each measuring 25cm/10in square
For the spice paste
  200g/7oz onion, chopped
  6 candlenuts
  15ml/1 tbsp ground coriander
  10ml/2 tsp chilli powder
  15g/½oz shrimp paste
  15g/½oz galangal, peeled and chopped
  5ml/1 tsp ground turmeric

1 To make the spice paste, grind all the ingredients together until fine using a mortar and pestle or a food processor. Mix with the lime leaves, salt and sugar and transfer to a bowl.

2 Add the lobster to the bowl and mix well with the spices. Add the eggs, oil and coconut cream and stir thoroughly. The consistency should be like that of softened butter.

3 Scald the banana leaves in boiling water to soften them, and drain. Lay each piece of leaf out on a flat surface and place 30–45ml/2–3 tbsp of the spiced lobster mixture in the centre, spreading it out until it is about 6mm/¼in thick.

4 Fold the opposite edges of the leaf over the filling and tuck in the sides to make a firm parcel.

5 Prepare a charcoal grill or preheat a grill (broiler) to high. Grill the banana leaf parcels for 8–10 minutes, turning once halfway through cooking. Serve immediately, to be unwrapped at the table.

COOK'S TIP
The coconut cream used in this recipe gives the fish mixture a thick, delicious and luscious consistency. Coconut cream can be taken from the top of a can of ordinary coconut milk that is available in most food stores, or may be taken from the first squeeze from freshly reconstituted desiccated coconut.

Per portion Energy 369Kcal/1531kJ; Protein 18.5g; Carbohydrate 8g, of which sugars 4.6g; Fat 29.7g, of which saturates 16.5g; Cholesterol 168mg; Calcium 119mg; Fibre 0.8g; Sodium 359mg.

SARAWAK SAMBAL UDANG

THIS VERSION OF THE MALAYSIAN DISH SAMBAL UDANG IS SIMPLE AND FIERY. TO ACCOMPANY THE DISH IN SARAWAK, YOU MIGHT BE OFFERED THE LOCAL, THICK SAGO PASTE, A BOWL OF STIR-FRIED FERN SHOOTS AND A LITTLE TUAK, THE HEADY, HOME-BREWED RICE WINE. THE DAYAKS, IBANS AND MELANAU ALSO COOK THE GRUBS FOUND IN SAGO PALMS IN THIS WAY.

SERVES FOUR

INGREDIENTS

- 8 shallots, chopped
- 4 garlic cloves, chopped
- 8–10 dried red chillies, soaked in warm water until soft, squeezed dry, seeded and chopped
- 5ml/1 tsp shrimp paste
- 30ml/2 tbsp vegetable or groundnut (peanut) oil
- 250ml/8fl oz/1 cup coconut cream
- 500g/1¼lb raw prawns (shrimp), peeled and deveined
- 10ml/2 tsp tamarind concentrate
- 15ml/1 tbsp palm sugar (jaggery)
- salt and ground black pepper
- 2 red chillies, seeded and finely chopped, and fresh coriander (cilantro) leaves, finely chopped, to garnish
- crusty bread or steamed rice and pickles, to serve

1 Using a mortar and pestle or food processor, grind the shallots, garlic and dried chillies to a coarse paste. Beat in the shrimp paste.

2 Heat the oil in a wok or heavy pan and stir in the paste until fragrant. Add the coconut cream and bubble it up until it separates. Toss in the prawns, reduce the heat and simmer for 3 minutes until the prawns have changed colour.

3 Stir in the tamarind concentrate and the sugar and cook for a further 2 minutes until the sauce is very thick. Season with salt and pepper and scatter the chopped chillies and coriander over the top. Serve immediately with chunks of fresh, crusty bread to mop up the sauce, or with steamed rice and pickles.

Per Portion Energy 330Kcal/1371kJ; Protein 25.9g; Carbohydrate 3.7g, of which sugars 3.2g; Fat 23.6g, of which saturates 15.6g; Cholesterol 263mg; Calcium 156mg; Fibre 0.4g; Sodium 408mg.

MALAY FISH CURRY

THE FISH CURRIES OF MALAYSIA DIFFER SLIGHTLY FROM REGION TO REGION, BUT MOST OF THEM INCLUDE A VARIETY OF INDIAN SPICES AND MANY ARE ENRICHED WITH COCONUT MILK. THE MALAY FOOD STALLS OFTEN FEATURE A FISH, CHICKEN OR BEEF CURRY, WHICH IS USUALLY SERVED WITH BREAD OR RICE, PICKLES AND EXTRA CHILLIES FOR THOSE WHO LIKE IT REALLY HOT.

1 To make the curry paste, use a mortar and pestle or food processor to grind the shallots, garlic, ginger, turmeric and chillies to a paste, transfer to a bowl and set aside.

2 Again, using the mortar and pestle or food processor, grind the roasted coriander and cumin seeds, the fish curry powder, fennel seeds and peppercorns to a powder. Add this mixture to the paste in the bowl. Bind with 15ml/1 tbsp water and thoroughly mix together.

3 Heat the oil in a wok or heavy pan. Stir in the curry paste and fry until fragrant. Stir in the tamarind concentrate. Add the fish and cook for 1 minute on each side.

4 Pour in the coconut milk, mix well and bring to the boil. Reduce the heat and simmer for 8–10 minutes until the fish is cooked.

5 Season to taste with salt. Scatter the coriander over the top and serve with plain or yellow rice, or with chunks of crusty bread to mop up the sauce.

SERVES FOUR

INGREDIENTS
30ml/2 tbsp vegetable oil
7.5ml/1½ tsp tamarind concentrate
8 thick fish cutlets, about 90g/3½oz each, such as grouper, red snapper, trout or mackerel
800ml/1½ pints coconut milk
salt
fresh coriander (cilantro) leaves, roughly chopped, to garnish
rice or crusty bread, to serve

For the curry paste
4 shallots, chopped
4 garlic cloves, chopped
50g/2oz fresh root ginger, peeled and chopped
25g/1oz fresh turmeric, chopped
4–6 dried red chillies, softened in warm water, seeded and chopped
15ml/1 tbsp coriander seeds, roasted
15ml/1 tbsp cumin seeds, roasted
10ml/2 tsp fish curry powder
5ml/1 tsp fennel seeds
2.5ml/½ tsp black peppercorns

COOK'S TIP
To roast the spices, heat them gently in a dry, heavy pan until they begin to colour and develop a nutty aroma. Take care not to burn them.

Per Portion Energy 264Kcal/1109kJ; Protein 36.6g; Carbohydrate 12.7g, of which sugars 12.1g; Fat 7.7g, of which saturates 1.3g; Cholesterol 89mg; Calcium 110mg; Fibre 1g; Sodium 354mg.

SABAHAN SQUID IN HOT YELLOW SAUCE

SIMPLE FISHERMEN'S DISHES SUCH AS THIS ONE ARE COOKED THE LENGTH AND BREADTH OF MALAYSIA'S COASTLINE. THIS RECIPE COMES FROM SABAH, THE NORTHERNMOST STATE IN MALAYSIAN BORNEO, AND INCLUDES ENOUGH CHILLIES TO SET YOUR TONGUE ON FIRE. THE DISH IS OFTEN SERVED WITH THE LOCAL STAPLE, SAGO PORRIDGE, AND SHREDDED GREEN MANGO TOSSED IN LIME JUICE.

SERVES FOUR

INGREDIENTS
  500g/1¼lb fresh squid
  juice of 2 limes
  5ml/1 tsp salt
  4 shallots, chopped
  4 garlic cloves, chopped
  25g/1oz galangal, chopped
  25g/1oz fresh turmeric, chopped
  6–8 red chillies, seeded and chopped
  30ml/2 tbsp vegetable or groundnut
    (peanut) oil
  7.5ml/1½ tsp palm sugar (jaggery)
  2 lemon grass stalks, crushed
  4 kaffir lime leaves
  400ml/14fl oz/1⅔ cups coconut milk
  salt and ground black pepper
  crusty bread or steamed rice,
    to serve

5 Drain the squid of any juice and toss it around the wok, coating it in the flavourings. Pour in the coconut milk and bring it to the boil. Reduce the heat and simmer for 5–10 minutes, until the squid is tender. Season with salt and pepper and serve with chunks of fresh, crusty bread or steamed rice.

1 First prepare the squid. Hold the body sac in one hand and pull off the head with the other. Sever the tentacles just above the eyes, and discard the rest of the head and innards. Clean the body sac inside and out with cold water and remove the skin.

2 Pat the squid dry, cut it into thick slices and put them in a bowl, along with the tentacles. Mix the lime juice with the salt and rub it into the squid. Set aside for 30 minutes.

3 Meanwhile, using a mortar and pestle or food processor, grind the shallots, garlic, galangal, turmeric and chillies to a coarse paste.

4 Heat the oil in a wok or heavy pan, and stir in the coarse paste. Cook the paste until fragrant, then stir in the palm sugar, lemon grass and whole kaffir lime leaves.

COOK'S TIP
Serve this spicy dish with some plain rice or fresh crusty bread to temper the heat of the chillies.

Per Portion Energy 185Kcal/780kJ; Protein 19.8g; Carbohydrate 9.4g, of which sugars 7.6g; Fat 8g, of which saturates 1.4g; Cholesterol 281mg; Calcium 50mg; Fibre 0.2g; Sodium 739mg.

MALAY COCKLE CURRY

THIS SEAFOOD CURRY IS QUITE FIERY, THE WAY THE MALAYS LIKE IT. IN THE TOWN OF KOTA BARU ON THE EAST COAST OF THE MALAY PENINSULA, THE HAWKER STALLS SELL A RANGE OF SPICY CURRIES AND, AS SEAFOOD IS VARIED AND ABUNDANT HERE, SHELLFISH TURN UP IN MANY OF THE DISHES. YOU CAN USE MUSSELS, COCKLES OR CLAMS IN THIS RECIPE.

SERVES FOUR

INGREDIENTS
- 500g/1¼lb cockles
- 45ml/3 tbsp vegetable oil
- 300m/½ pint/1¼ cups coconut milk
- 30ml/2 tbsp lime juice
- 5ml/1 tsp salt
- 2 tomatoes, quartered
- small sprig sweet basil, plus extra to garnish

For the spice paste
- ½ large onion, chopped
- 5 garlic cloves, chopped
- 15ml/1 tbsp fresh root ginger, peeled
- 5 red chillies, seeded and chopped
- 15ml/1 tbsp ground coriander
- 10ml/2 tsp ground cumin
- 15g/½oz shrimp paste

1 Wash and shell the cockles.

2 Grate the ginger and grind all the ingredients for the spice paste using a pestle and mortar or a food processor.

3 Heat the oil in a wok or pan and fry the paste for 2–3 minutes until fragrant. Add the coconut milk, lime juice and salt and simmer for 5 minutes.

4 Add the cockles, tomatoes and basil and cook over a medium heat for 3 more minutes.

5 Serve hot in warmed bowls, garnished with more sweet basil sprigs.

COOK'S TIP
To this basic curry can be added extra ingredients such as diced pineapple, cucumber or sour star fruit (carambola).

Per portion Energy 198Kcal/832kJ; Protein 18.8g; Carbohydrate 8.6g, of which sugars 6.1g; Fat 10.3g, of which saturates 1.6g; Cholesterol 85mg; Calcium 199mg; Fibre 0.7g; Sodium 865mg.

MEAT AND POULTRY

The meat dishes of Malaysia divide along ethnic lines, as the types of meat eaten are subject to the different dietary codes of Islam, Hinduism and Buddhism. Malay dishes tend to mainly concentrate on beef, mutton or goat, as Muslims do not eat pork, whereas chicken is a staple of the diet. Duck is also popular too, with the universally loved Cantonese Roast Duck being a particular favourite.

HAINANESE CHICKEN RICE

THIS HAINANESE-DERIVED RECIPE FOCUSES ON AN UNUSUAL STEEPING PROCESS TO ENSURE SMOOTH, SILKY CHICKEN, WHICH IS ACCOMPANIED BY AROMATIC RICE, A BOWL OF CHICKEN BROTH, SOY SAUCE FOR DIPPING AND A GARNISH OF CRUNCHY SPRING ONIONS AND CUCUMBER. WITH THEIR PREFERENCE FOR HOT TASTES, THE MALAYS ADD A PUNGENT GINGER AND CHILLI DIPPING SAUCE.

SERVES FOUR TO SIX

INGREDIENTS
- 1 chicken (1.25kg/2½lb), cleaned
- 30ml/2 tbsp light soy sauce
- 15ml/1 tbsp Chinese rice wine
- 50g/2oz fresh root ginger, peeled, thickly sliced and crushed
- 4 garlic cloves, lightly crushed
- 2 spring onions (scallions), crushed
- 1.5 litres/2½ pints/ 6¼ cups chicken stock
- 10ml/2 tsp sesame oil
- 225g/8oz/generous 1 cup jasmine rice, rinsed and drained
- salt and ground black pepper

For the sambal
- 10 red chillies, seeded and chopped
- 6 garlic cloves, chopped
- 25g/1oz fresh root ginger, peeled and chopped
- 15ml/1 tbsp sesame or groundnut (peanut) oil
- 15–30ml/1–2 tbsp fresh lime juice
- 10ml/2 tsp sugar
- 2.5ml/½ tsp salt

For the garnish
- fresh coriander (cilantro) leaves
- dark soy sauce
- 1 small cucumber, halved lengthways and finely sliced
- 3 spring onions, trimmed and sliced

1 Rub the chicken, inside and out, with 15ml/1 tbsp soy sauce and the rice wine. Place the ginger, garlic and spring onions in the cavity. Leave to stand for 30 minutes.

COOK'S TIP
Adopted from the Hainan communities that settled in Malaysia and Singapore, this dish has become a classic in both regions. It is cooked in the home, and served at hawker stalls, coffee shops and restaurants, but the best places to sample this dish are the chicken rice shops, where it is cooked daily following age-old methods.

2 Put the chicken stock in a large pan and bring to the boil.

3 Immerse the chicken in the boiling stock. Bring back to the boil, cover the pan and turn off the heat.

4 Leave the chicken to steep for 15 minutes. Lift the chicken to drain the cavity, reheat the stock to boiling point, cover the pan and steep the chicken in the stock, off the heat, for a further 15 minutes. Repeat the process every 15 minutes, until the chicken has steeped for a total of 1 hour.

5 Lift the chicken out of the stock, allowing the juices to drip back into the pan, and plunge it into a bowl of iced water. Bring the stock back to the boil. Drain the chicken, trim off the wings, neck and legs, and add to the stock. Rub the remaining 15ml/1 tbsp soy sauce and the sesame oil over the chicken and set aside.

6 Keep the stock simmering, skim off any fat from the top and season. Measure 550ml/18fl oz/2½ cups of the stock and pour into a separate pan (cover the remaining stock and keep it barely simmering).

7 Bring the measured stock to the boil and add the rice. Stir once, reduce the heat and simmer until the stock is absorbed. Turn off the heat, cover the pan with a dish towel, then the lid, and leave to stand for 15 minutes.

8 Meanwhile, prepare the sambal. Using a mortar and pestle or food processor, grind the chillies, garlic and ginger to a smooth paste. Bind with the oil and lime juice, and stir in the sugar and salt. Spoon the sambal into individual dipping bowls.

9 To serve, first joint the chicken. Remove the skin and separate the meat from the bones. Slice the thighs and breasts into bitesize pieces. Place the chicken on a platter and garnish with a few coriander leaves.

10 Pack spoonfuls of the rice into a small bowl and invert one on to each plate. Place the bowls of sambal on each plate, along with individual bowls of dark soy sauce, slices of cucumber and a few coriander leaves.

11 Ladle the hot chicken broth into bowls and sprinkle spring onions on top. Place a plate of rice and sauces, and bowl of broth, in front of each person, and set the chicken in the middle of the table.

Per Portion Energy 460Kcal/1913kJ; Protein 28.6g; Carbohydrate 30.4g, of which sugars 0.4g; Fat 24.6g, of which saturates 6.7g; Cholesterol 133mg; Calcium 37mg; Fibre 0.5g; Sodium 108mg.

MALAYSIAN FRIED CHICKEN

IF YOU VISIT MALAYSIA, THEN IT WOULD BE ALMOST UNTHINKABLE NOT TO SAMPLE THE FAMOUS FRIED CHICKEN. INDONESIAN IN ORIGIN, AYAM GORENG PUTS WESTERN FRIED CHICKEN TO SHAME. FIRST THE CHICKEN IS COOKED IN SPICES AND FLAVOURINGS TO ENSURE A DEPTH OF FLAVOUR, THEN IT IS SIMPLY DEEP-FRIED TO FORM A CRISP, GOLDEN SKIN.

SERVES FOUR

INGREDIENTS

2 shallots, chopped
4 garlic cloves, chopped
50g/2oz fresh root ginger or
  galangal, chopped
25g/1oz fresh turmeric, chopped
2 lemon grass stalks, chopped
12 chicken thighs or drumsticks or
  6 whole chicken legs, separated
  into drumsticks and thighs
30ml/2 tbsp kecap manis
salt and ground black pepper
vegetable oil, for deep-frying

1 Using a mortar and pestle or food processor, grind the shallots, garlic, ginger or galangal, turmeric and lemon grass to a paste.

COOK'S TIP
Served with a sambal, or pickle, ayam goreng makes a delicious snack, but for a main course serve it with yellow or fragrant coconut rice and a salad. If you cannot find kecap manis, use soy sauce sweetened with palm sugar, available in Chinese and Asian markets, or substitute the same quantity of dark soy sauce and 15ml/1 tbsp sugar.

2 Place the chicken pieces in a heavy pan or earthenware pot and smear with the spice paste. Add the kecap manis and 150ml/¼ pint/⅔ cup water. Bring to the boil, reduce the heat and cook the chicken for about 25 minutes, turning it from time to time, until the liquid has evaporated. The chicken should be dry before deep-frying, but the spices should be sticking to it. Season with salt and pepper.

3 Heat enough oil for deep-frying in a wok. Fry the chicken pieces in batches until golden brown and crisp. Drain them on kitchen paper and serve hot.

Per Portion Energy 396Kcal/1639kJ; Protein 27g; Carbohydrate 1.5g, of which sugars 1.1g; Fat 31.3g, of which saturates 6.8g; Cholesterol 150mg; Calcium 38mg; Fibre 0.2g; Sodium 358mg.

DEVIL'S CURRY

THIS EURASIAN DISH, KNOWN AS CURRY DEBAL, REALLY IS DEVILISHLY HOT. EVERY EURASIAN HOUSEHOLD HAS ITS OWN VERSION OF THIS CHICKEN AND VEGETABLE HOTPOT WITH A FIERY, SOUR SAUCE. SERVED AS A MEAL ON ITS OWN, WITH BREAD TO MOP UP THE SAUCE, IT IS OFTEN COOKED FOR FAMILY CELEBRATIONS. YOU CAN LESSEN THE CHILLI CONTENT IF YOU WISH.

SERVES SIX

INGREDIENTS
  4–6 chicken breasts or 12 boned
    chicken thighs, cut into bitesize
    chunks
  60ml/4 tbsp vegetable oil
  1 onion, halved lengthways, and
    sliced along the grain
  25g/1oz fresh root ginger, peeled and
    cut into julienne strips
  4 garlic cloves, cut into strips
  30–45ml/2–3 tbsp vinegar
  10ml/2 tsp sugar
  3 medium potatoes, cut into bitesize
    chunks
  2 courgettes (zucchini), partially
    peeled, halved lengthways, seeded
    and cut into bitesize chunks
  8 Chinese leaves (Chinese cabbage),
    cut into bitesize squares
  10ml/2 tsp brown mustard seeds,
    ground and mixed to a paste with
    a little water
  salt
  crusty bread, to serve
For the spice paste
  10 dried chillies, soaked in warm
    water until soft, squeezed dry and
    seeded
  6 fresh red chillies, seeded and
    chopped
  8 shallots, chopped
  6 garlic cloves, chopped
  25g/1oz fresh root ginger, peeled
    and chopped
  6 candlenuts or macadamia nuts
  10ml/2 tsp ground turmeric
For the marinade
  15ml/1 tbsp light soy sauce
  15ml/1 tbsp dark soy sauce
  10ml/2 tsp rice or white wine vinegar
  10ml/2 tsp sugar

COOK'S TIP
The flavour of this curry improves if it is made a day in advance. Cool it quickly then store in the refrigerator overnight to allow the flavours to mingle. Reheat the following day.

1 For the spice paste, grind the chillies, shallots, garlic, ginger and nuts. Stir in the turmeric and set aside.

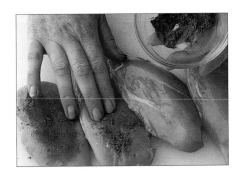

2 Mix together the marinade ingredients and rub it into the chicken pieces. Leave to marinate for 30 minutes.

3 Heat the oil in a wok or heavy pan. Stir in the onion, ginger and garlic and fry until golden. Add the spice paste and stir until fragrant. Toss in the marinated chicken and stir until it begins to brown, then pour in enough water to cover.

4 Bring to the boil and add the vinegar, sugar and potatoes. Reduce the heat and cook gently until the potatoes are tender when tested with a sharp knife.

5 Add the courgettes and cook for 2 minutes, then stir in the cabbage. Stir in the mustard paste and season with salt. Serve hot with bread.

Per Portion Energy 270Kcal/1136kJ; Protein 32.5g; Carbohydrate 15.4g, of which sugars 4.6g; Fat 9.1g, of which saturates 1.3g; Cholesterol 88mg; Calcium 36mg; Fibre 1.8g; Sodium 441mg.

CURRY KAPITAN <u>WITH</u> COCONUT <u>AND</u> CHILLI RELISH

CURRY KAPITAN RECALLS THE TRADITIONAL ROLE OF THE CHINESE KAPITAN, A MAN OF CONSIDERABLE SOCIAL STANDING AMONG THE MALAY AND CHINESE PEOPLE IN OLD MELAKA. IT IS SAID TO BE A DISH INVENTED BY THE PERANAKANS, PERHAPS TO PRESENT TO THE KAPITAN OR TO CELEBRATE HIS ROLE. A CHICKEN CURRY, MADE WITH COCONUT MILK, IT OWES ITS FLAVOUR TO ALL THE INHABITANTS OF OLD MELAKA THROUGH ITS USE OF SPICES AND FLAVOURINGS — CHINESE, MALAY, PORTUGUESE AND INDIAN — AND COULD BE REGARDED AS MELAKA IN A POT.

SERVES FOUR

INGREDIENTS

For the rempah
  6–8 dried red chillies, soaked in
    warm water until soft, squeezed dry
    and seeded
  6–8 shallots, chopped
  4–6 garlic cloves, chopped
  25g/1oz fresh root ginger, chopped
  5ml/1 tsp shrimp paste
  10ml/2 tsp ground turmeric
  10ml/2 tsp Chinese
    five-spice powder
For the curry
  15–30ml/1–2 tbsp tamarind pulp
  1 fresh coconut, grated (shredded)
  30–45ml/2–3 tbsp vegetable or
    groundnut (peanut) oil
  1–2 cinnamon sticks
  12 chicken thighs, boned and cut
    into bitesize strips lengthways
  600ml/1 pint/2½ cups coconut milk
  15ml/1 tbsp palm sugar (jaggery)
  salt and ground black pepper

For the relish
  1 green chilli, seeded and finely sliced
  1 red chilli, seeded and finely sliced
  fresh coriander (cilantro) leaves,
    finely chopped (reserve a few leaves
    for garnishing)
  2 limes
  steamed rice, to serve

1 First make the rempah. Using a mortar and pestle or food processor, grind the chillies, shallots, garlic and ginger to a paste. Beat in the shrimp paste and stir in the dried spices.

2 Soak the tamarind pulp in 150ml/ ¼ pint/⅔ cup warm water until soft. Squeeze the pulp to soften it, then strain to extract the juice and discard the pulp.

3 In a heavy pan, dry roast half the grated coconut over a medium heat until it is just turning golden brown and emits a nutty aroma. Be careful not to burn it.

4 Using a mortar and pestle or food processor, grind the roasted coconut until it resembles sugar grains.

COOK'S TIP
Palm sugar lends a unique, caramelized flavour to the dish. As a substitute, you could try muscovado sugar.

5 Heat the oil in a wok or earthenware pot, and stir in the rempah and cinnamon sticks until fragrant. Add the chicken strips.

6 Pour in the coconut milk and tamarind water, and stir in the sugar. Reduce the heat and cook gently for about 10 minutes. Stir in half the ground roasted coconut and season.

7 In a bowl, mix the remaining grated coconut with the chillies, coriander and juice of 1 lime to serve as a relish.

8 Cut the other lime into wedges. Spoon the chicken curry into a serving dish and garnish with a few coriander leaves. Serve with the coconut and chilli relish, the lime wedges to squeeze over it and a bowl of steamed rice.

Per Portion Energy 487Kcal/2024kJ; Protein 29.2g; Carbohydrate 11.3g, of which sugars 10.6g; Fat 36.4g, of which saturates 19.2g; Cholesterol 150mg; Calcium 114mg; Fibre 4.4g; Sodium 267mg.

MALAY BRAISED DUCK ^{IN} AROMATIC SAUCE

THE CHINESE COMMUNITIES IN MALAYSIA OFTEN BRAISE DUCK, GOOSE, CHICKEN OR PORK IN SOY SAUCE AND WARM FLAVOURINGS, SUCH AS STAR ANISE AND CINNAMON. SUCH DISHES ARE FOUND AT CHINESE HAWKER STALLS AND COFFEE SHOPS, AND THERE ARE MANY VARIATIONS ON THE THEME. THE MALAYS LIKE TO ADD TURMERIC AND LEMON GRASS TO THE FLAVOURINGS AND, TO ACHIEVE THEIR DESIRED FIERY KICK, CHILLIES ARE ALWAYS TUCKED INTO THE RECIPE SOMEWHERE.

SERVES FOUR TO SIX

INGREDIENTS

1 duck (about 2kg/4½ lb), washed
  and trimmed
15–30ml/1–2 tbsp Chinese
  five-spice powder
25g/1oz fresh turmeric, chopped
25g/1oz galangal, chopped
4 garlic cloves, chopped
30ml/2 tbsp sesame oil
12 shallots, peeled and left whole
2–3 lemon grass stalks, halved and
  lightly crushed
4 cinnamon sticks
8 star anise
12 cloves
600ml/1 pint/2½ cups light soy sauce
120ml/4fl oz/½ cup dark soy sauce
30–45ml/2–3 tbsp palm sugar (jaggery)
coriander (cilantro) leaves, to garnish
  2 green and 2 red chillies,
  seeded and quartered lengthways,
  to garnish
steamed jasmine rice and salad,
  to serve

1 Rub the duck, inside and out, with the five-spice powder and place in the refrigerator, uncovered, for 6–8 hours to absorb the flavours.

2 Using a mortar and pestle or food processor, grind the turmeric, galangal and garlic to a smooth paste. Heat the oil in a heavy pan and stir in the spice paste until it becomes fragrant. Stir in the shallots, lemon grass, cinnamon sticks, star anise and cloves. Pour in the soy sauces and stir in the sugar until dissolved.

3 Place the duck in the pan, baste with the sauce, and add 550ml/18fl oz/ 2½ cups water. Bring to the boil, reduce the heat and cover the pan. Simmer gently for 4–6 hours, basting from time to time, until the duck is very tender. Garnish with coriander and chillies, and serve with rice and salad.

Per Portion Energy 119Kcal/498kJ; Protein 10.2g; Carbohydrate 4.6g, of which sugars 3.4g; Fat 6.9g, of which saturates 1.5g; Cholesterol 50mg; Calcium 35mg; Fibre 1.1g; Sodium 412mg.

CANTONESE ROAST DUCK

POSSIBLY ONE OF THE BEST KNOWN DUCK DISHES AROUND THE WORLD, THIS SITS NEXT TO THE OTHER TWO UNIVERSALLY ACCLAIMED DISHES, PEKING DUCK AND CRISPY AROMATIC DUCK, AS A GRAND BANQUET DISH. THE BEST ROAST DUCK SHOULD HAVE REALLY CRACKLY, CRISP SKIN AND FOR THIS, THE TRADITIONAL METHOD USED IN CHINESE COOKING TO PREPARE PEKING DUCK IS TO DRY THE DUCK IN THE SUN FOR AT LEAST SIX HOURS BEFORE COOKING.

SERVES SIX TO EIGHT

INGREDIENTS

    1 prepared duck (about 1.5kg/3½lb),
      trimmed of excess fat
    30ml/2 tbsp hoisin sauce
    30ml/2 tbsp Chinese rice wine
      or sherry
    1 small cube preserved red soy bean,
      mashed fine
    few drops cochineal, or red food
      colouring

1 Tie a length of string under the wings and around the neck of the duck to make a loop.

2 Fill a large pan with water and bring to the boil.

3 Hold the string around the duck and immerse it several times to shrink the skin and remove some of the fat.

4 Hang up the duck in a clean and an airy spot for several hours, if possible for the whole day if you are cooking it in the evening. During this time, the skin will take on a parchment-like texture as it dries out.

COOK'S TIPS
• Unlike chicken, duck may be eaten slightly pink in the middle.
• You can buy various chilli sauces in any supermarket. This dish goes well with a sweet chilli dip, or you could serve it with plum sauce.

5 Preheat the oven to 220°C/425°F/ Gas 7. Blend the hoisin sauce with the wine, preserved red soy bean and red colouring and rub it all over the duck.

6 Place the duck on a rack in a large roasting pan and roast for 30 minutes. Reduce the heat to 180°C/350°F/Gas 4 and cook for another 30 minutes. Push a metal skewer into the deepest part between the thigh and breast – if the juice runs clear the duck is done.

7 Turn off the heat and leave the duck in the oven for 20 minutes to continue cooking in the residual heat.

8 Chop the duck into serving pieces and serve with sliced cucumber and a chilli sauce dip.

Per portion Energy 384kcal/1581kJ; Protein 10g; Carbohydrate 0.7g, of which sugars 0.7g; Fat 37.4g, of which saturates 10.2g; Cholesterol 0mg; Calcium 11mg; Fibre 0g; Sodium 232mg.

RENDANG

IN THE 15TH CENTURY, WHEN THE MINANGKABAU PEOPLE FIRST CAME FROM SUMATRA TO SETTLE IN THE SMALL STATE OF NEGERI SEMBILAN, THEY BROUGHT WITH THEM THEIR TRADITIONAL SOCIAL CUSTOMS AND FIERY COOKING STYLES. ALTHOUGH THE CUSTOMS HAVE BEEN DILUTED OVER TIME, MANY OF THE UNIQUE DISHES HAVE SURVIVED, AND RENDANG IS ONE OF THEM. MADE WITH BEEF OR, TRADITIONALLY, WITH THE MEAT OF WATER BUFFALO, THIS DISH MUST BE SLOW-COOKED TO ACHIEVE THE REQUIRED TENDERNESS AND TO REDUCE THE SAUCE TO A SYRUPY THICKNESS.

SERVES SIX

INGREDIENTS

- 1kg/2¼lb beef topside (pot roast) or rump (round) steak, cut into bitesize cubes
- 115g/4oz fresh coconut, grated, or 50g/2oz desiccated (dry unsweetened shredded) coconut
- 15ml/1 tbsp tamarind pulp, soaked in 90ml/6 tbsp water until soft
- 45ml/3 tbsp vegetable or groundnut (peanut) oil
- 2 onions, halved lengthways, and sliced along the grain
- 3 lemon grass stalks, trimmed, halved and bruised
- 2 cinnamon sticks
- 1.2 litres/2 pints/5 cups coconut milk
- 15ml/1 tbsp sugar
- salt and ground black pepper
- steamed rice or bread and salad, to serve

For the spice paste
- 8–10 dried red chillies, soaked in warm water until soft, squeezed dry and seeded
- 8 shallots, chopped
- 4–6 garlic cloves, chopped
- 50g/2oz fresh galangal, chopped
- 25g/1oz fresh turmeric, chopped
- 15ml/1 tbsp coriander seeds
- 10ml/2 tsp cumin seeds
- 5ml/1 tsp black peppercorns

COOK'S TIP

In Malaysia, rendang is often served with *roti jala* to mop up the deliciously rich sauce. These are thin Indian pancakes made with coconut milk. They have a lacy, net-like appearance, which is achieved by swirling a small amount of the batter around in a hot pan.

1 First make the spice paste. Using a mortar and pestle or food processor, grind the soaked chillies, shallots, garlic, galangal and turmeric to a smooth paste.

2 In a small heavy pan, dry-roast the coriander and cumin seeds with the peppercorns, until they start to give off a nutty aroma. Grind the roasted spices to a powder and stir this into the spice paste.

3 Coat the beef in the spice paste and set aside to marinate for about 1 hour.

4 Meanwhile, dry-roast the grated coconut in a heavy pan, until it is brown and emits a nutty aroma.

5 Using a mortar and pestle or food processor, grind the roasted coconut until it resembles brown sugar and set it aside.

6 Squeeze the tamarind to help soften it, then strain it to extract the juice. Discard the pulp.

7 Heat the oil in a wok or heavy pan. Add the onions, lemon grass and cinnamon sticks, and fry until the onions begin to colour. Add the beef with all the spice paste and toss it around the wok, until lightly browned.

8 Pour the coconut milk and tamarind juice into the pan and bring to the boil, stirring all the time. Reduce the heat and simmer gently, until the sauce begins to thicken.

9 Stir in the sugar and the ground roasted coconut, and continue to simmer very gently, stirring from time to time, until the meat is tender and the reduced sauce is very thick. This may take 2–4 hours, depending on the cut and type of meat.

10 Season with salt and black pepper to taste, and serve hot with rice or bread and a salad.

Per Portion Energy 439Kcal/1842kJ; Protein 41g; Carbohydrate 19.4g, of which sugars 17.4g; Fat 22.7g, of which saturates 13.1g; Cholesterol 83mg; Calcium 94mg; Fibre 3.8g; Sodium 356mg.

OXTAIL IN HOT TANGY SAUCE

CONSIDERED A DELICACY IN SOME PARTS OF SOUTH-EAST ASIA, OXTAIL AND THE TAILS OF WATER BUFFALO ARE GENERALLY COOKED FOR SPECIAL FEASTS AND CELEBRATIONS. OXTAIL IS COOKED IN EUROPEAN-STYLE STEWS BY THE EURASIANS AND HAINANESE, BUT THE MALAYS AND INDONESIANS PREFER TO COOK IT SLOWLY IN A HOT, TANGY SAUCE. SERVED WITH STEAMED RICE, OR CHUNKS OF FRESH, CRUSTY BREAD, IT MAKES A VERY TASTY SUPPER DISH.

SERVES FOUR TO SIX

INGREDIENTS

8 shallots, chopped
8 garlic cloves, chopped
4–6 red chillies, seeded and chopped
25g/1oz fresh galangal, chopped
30ml/2 tbsp rice flour or plain (all-purpose) flour
15ml/1 tbsp ground turmeric
8–12 oxtail joints, cut roughly the same size and trimmed of fat
45ml/3 tbsp vegetable oil
400g/14oz can plum tomatoes, drained
2 lemon grass stalks, halved and bruised
a handful of fresh kaffir lime leaves
225g/8oz tamarind pulp, soaked in 600ml/1 pint/2½ cups water, squeezed and strained
30–45ml/2–3 tbsp sugar
salt and ground black pepper
fresh coriander (cilantro) leaves, roughly chopped

1 Using a mortar and pestle or food processor, grind the shallots, garlic, chillies and galangal to a coarse paste. Mix the flour with the ground turmeric and spread it on a flat surface or a large plate. Roll the oxtail in the flour to coat thoroughly and set aside.

2 Heat the oil in a heavy pan or earthenware pot. Stir in the spice paste and cook until fragrant and golden. Add the oxtail joints and brown on all sides. Add the tomatoes, lemon grass stalks, lime leaves and tamarind juice. Add enough water to cover the oxtail, and bring it to the boil. Skim off any fat from the surface. Reduce the heat, put the lid on the pan and simmer the oxtail for about 2 hours.

3 Stir in the sugar, season to taste with salt and pepper and continue to cook, uncovered, for a further 30–40 minutes, until the meat is very tender.

4 Sprinkle with the coriander and serve straight from the pan.

Per Portion Energy 386Kcal/1611kJ; Protein 34.5g; Carbohydrate 11.3g, of which sugars 6.6g; Fat 22.6g, of which saturates 7.7g; Cholesterol 125mg; Calcium 31mg; Fibre 1.2g; Sodium 191mg.

BEEF SEMUR

THE INDONESIAN-COINED TERM SEMUR OR SMOOR, ALSO USED IN MALAYSIA, REFERS TO ANY DISH COOKED IN SOY SAUCE IN TANDEM WITH A TART SEASONING SUCH AS TAMARIND OR LIME JUICE. THIS IS A DRY DISH THAT TASTES EVEN BETTER A DAY OR TWO AFTER IT IS MADE. USE A FAIRLY TENDER CUT OF BEEF SUCH AS SIRLOIN, RUMP OR EVEN JAPANESE-CUT SUKIYAKI BEEF TO REDUCE THE COOKING TIME, ALTHOUGH TRADITIONALLY INDONESIANS USE TOUGHER CUTS, COOKED SLOWLY.

SERVES FOUR

INGREDIENTS
600g/1lb 6oz beef sirloin or rump
(round) steak
30ml/2 tbsp dark soy sauce
15ml/1 tbsp lime juice
45ml/3 tbsp vegetable or groundnut
(peanut) oil
1 large onion, chopped
30ml/2 tbsp tamarind
concentrate
600ml/1 pint/2½ cups water
5 cloves
5ml/1 tsp salt
5ml/1 tsp sugar
For the spice paste
15ml/1 tbsp ground coriander
5ml/1 tsp ground cumin
5ml/1 tsp ground fennel
3 candlenuts
10ml/2 tsp black peppercorns

1 Slice the beef 1cm/½in thick. Whisk the soy sauce and lime juice together, pour over the beef in a non-metallic container and marinate for half an hour.

2 Heat the oil in a wok or heavy pan and fry the onion for 2 minutes, until softened. Blend the ground spices for the spice paste with a little water then add the remaining ingredients and grind to a paste.

3 Add the spice paste to the pan and fry for 2 minutes. Add the beef with its marinade, the tamarind, water, cloves, salt and sugar. Reduce the heat and simmer, covered, for 40 minutes.

4 At the end of the cooking time the liquid should have reduced by half. Remove the beef to a serving plate. Correct the seasoning if necessary and serve the gravy on the side.

Per portion Energy 400Kcal/1664kJ; Protein 36.7g; Carbohydrate 11.1g, of which sugars 5.8g; Fat 23.7g, of which saturates 6.9g; Cholesterol 87mg; Calcium 46mg; Fibre 1.1g; Sodium 1127mg.

SIZZLING LAMB WITH WINE SAUCE

THIS IS A WELL-KNOWN RESTAURANT DISH IN MALAYSIA, WHERE IT IS SERVED WITH PANACHE IN A CAST IRON HOT PLATE MOUNTED ON A WOODEN BASE. OF NORTH CHINESE ORIGIN, IT IS STEEPED IN CHINESE WINE, GINGER JUICE AND SESAME OIL AND IS USUALLY SERVED AS A WINTER WARMER.

SERVES FOUR

INGREDIENTS
    500g/1¼lb lean lamb
    45ml/3 tbsp ginger wine
    45ml/2 tbsp sesame oil
    2.5ml/½ tsp black pepper
    30ml/2 tbsp oyster sauce
    30ml/2 tbsp vegetable or groundnut
      (peanut) oil
    25g/1oz grated fresh root ginger
    4 garlic cloves, crushed
    3 spring onions (scallions), chopped
    10ml/2 tsp cornflour (cornstarch)

1 Cut the lamb into thin strips and tenderize by beating them with the blunt edge of a cleaver or meat mallet.

2 Blend the ginger wine with the sesame oil, pepper and oyster sauce and stir well to incorporate. Set aside. Heat the oil and fry the ginger and garlic for 2 minutes until they are just starting to brown.

3 Add the lamb strips and stir-fry for 3 minutes. Add the ginger wine mixture and bring to a fast boil. When the lamb is nearly done, add the chopped spring onions and stir for 1 minute. Blend the cornflour with a little water to make a smooth paste and add to the pan. Stir until the sauce is thick.

4 If you have a cast iron plate, heat it over a flame for 5 minutes and replace it on the wooden base, being careful to handle it with special tongs. Heap the lamb on the hot plate and serve immediately as the sizzling will die down very quickly.

COOK'S TIP
If you cannot find ginger wine, then grind a thumb-sized piece of fresh root ginger and blend this with 30ml/2 tbsp of Chinese Rice Wine.

Per portion Energy 386Kcal/1607kJ; Protein 24.9g; Carbohydrate 6.5g, of which sugars 4.1g; Fat 27.8g, of which saturates 8.4g; Cholesterol 95mg; Calcium 17mg; Fibre 0.2g; Sodium 294mg.

MALAY LAMB KORMA

ADAPTED FROM THE TRADITIONAL INDIAN KORMA, THE CREAMY MALAY VERSION IS FLAVOURED WITH COCONUT MILK. SERVED AT THE MALAY AND MUSLIM HAWKER STALLS, THIS TASTY LAMB KORMA IS OFTEN ACCOMPANIED BY FRAGRANT RICE OR FLATBREAD AND A MALAY SALAD OR SAMBAL.

SERVES FOUR TO SIX

INGREDIENTS
  25g/1oz fresh root ginger, peeled and chopped
  4 garlic cloves, chopped
  2 red chillies, seeded and chopped
  10ml/2 tsp garam masala
  10ml/2 tsp ground coriander
  5ml/1 tsp ground cumin
  5ml/1 tsp ground turmeric
  675g/1½lb lamb shoulder, cut into bitesize cubes
  45ml/3 tbsp ghee, or 30ml/2 tbsp vegetable oil and 15g/½oz/1 tbsp butter
  2 onions, halved lengthways and sliced along the grain
  2.5ml/½ tsp sugar
  4–6 cardamom pods, bruised
  1 cinnamon stick
  400ml/14fl oz/1⅔ cups coconut milk
  salt and ground black pepper
  30ml/2 tbsp roasted peanuts, crushed, and fresh coriander (cilantro) and mint leaves, coarsely chopped, to garnish

1 Using a mortar and pestle or food processor, grind the ginger, garlic and chillies to a paste. Stir in the garam masala, ground coriander, cumin and turmeric. Put the lamb into a shallow dish and rub the paste into it. Cover and leave to marinate for 1 hour.

2 Heat the ghee or oil and butter in a heavy pan or flameproof earthenware pot. Add the onions and sugar, and cook until brown and almost caramelized. Stir in the cardamom pods and cinnamon stick and add the lamb with all the marinade. Mix well and cook until the meat is browned all over.

3 Pour in the coconut milk, stir well and bring to the boil. Reduce the heat, cover the pan and cook gently for 30–40 minutes until the meat is tender. Make sure the meat doesn't become dry – stir in a little extra coconut milk, or water, if necessary.

4 Season to taste with salt and pepper. Scatter the peanuts over the top and garnish with the coriander and mint. Serve immediately.

COOK'S TIP
Homemade clarified butter can be used in place of ghee.

Per Portion Energy 267Kcal/1117kJ; Protein 24.3g; Carbohydrate 8.5g, of which sugars 6.8g; Fat 15.4g, of which saturates 6.4g; Cholesterol 86mg; Calcium 46mg; Fibre 1.2g; Sodium 211mg.

SARAWAK GOAT CURRY

GIVEN THEIR PROXIMITY, IT IS NO SURPRISE THAT SARAWAK, SABAH AND INDONESIA SHARE MANY DISHES, ALTHOUGH THERE ARE REGIONAL OR TRIBAL VARIATIONS ON A THEME. ONE THING THEY ALL HAVE IN COMMON IS THEIR ENJOYMENT OF MUTTON AND GOAT, WHICH THEY USUALLY COOK IN A CURRY OR CHARGRILL AS A SPICY SATAY. IN SARAWAK, THIS CURRY WOULD NORMALLY BE SERVED WITH THE LOCAL SAGO PORRIDGE, BUT IT IS EQUALLY DELICIOUS SERVED WITH STEAMED JASMINE RICE, AN INDIAN PILAFF OR CHUNKS OF FRESH CRUSTY BREAD AND A GREEN MANGO OR PAPAYA SALAD.

SERVES FOUR

INGREDIENTS

30ml/2 tbsp vegetable or groundnut (peanut) oil

2 cinnamon sticks

1kg/2¼lb lean goat meat, from the leg or shoulder, cut into bitesize strips

4 tomatoes, skinned, seeded and chopped

15–30ml/1–2 tbsp palm sugar (jaggery)

900ml/1½ pints/ 3¾ cups coconut milk

a handful of kaffir lime leaves

salt

fresh coriander (cilantro) leaves, roughly chopped, to garnish

3–4 green chillies, seeded and quartered lengthways, and bread, to serve

For the spice paste

8 shallots, chopped

6 garlic cloves, chopped

4 red chillies, seeded and chopped

50g/2oz galangal, chopped

25g/1oz fresh turmeric, chopped

2 lemon grass stalks, trimmed and chopped

4 candlenuts or macadamia nuts

15ml/1 tbsp coriander seeds

5ml/1 tsp cumin seeds

1 First make the spice paste. Using a mortar and pestle or food processor, grind the shallots, garlic, chillies, galangal, turmeric, lemon grass and nuts to a coarse paste. Grind the coriander and cumin seeds separately and stir them into the spice paste.

2 Heat the oil in a wok and stir in the spice paste. Add the cinnamon sticks. Once they start to emit a fragrant aroma, add the strips of goat, tossing them around the wok to brown them lightly. Stir in the tomatoes with the sugar and cook for 2 minutes before pouring in the coconut milk. Bring to the boil, stir in the lime leaves and reduce the heat.

3 Cover and simmer gently for about 1½ hours, until the meat is tender. Add more coconut milk if necessary to prevent the curry becoming too dry. Season to taste with salt, sprinkle with coriander and serve with chillies and crusty bread.

Per Portion Energy 625Kcal/2614kJ; Protein 51.3g; Carbohydrate 19.8g, of which sugars 19.2g; Fat 38.5g, of which saturates 14.7g; Cholesterol 190mg; Calcium 126mg; Fibre 2g; Sodium 88mg.

PENANG SPRING ROLLS

THESE SPRING ROLLS, WHICH ARE CALLED CHUEN PIAH, ARE A SPECIALITY OF PENANG COOKING. THEIR GENERIC NAME DOES THEM LITTLE JUSTICE, AS THEY ARE QUITE DIFFERENT FROM THE CHINESE VARIETY OF SPRING ROLL. COMMONLY CALLED LOBAK, THEY ARE ACTUALLY A MEAT-FILLED VERSION OF POPIAH, USING TOFU (BEAN CURD) INSTEAD OF FLOUR WRAPPERS. AS THE ROLLS REQUIRE A COARSELY GROUND PORK, IT'S ESSENTIAL TO CHOP THE MEAT YOURSELF, RATHER THAN USING SUPERMARKET MINCE, TO MAKE SURE YOU GET THE CORRECT TEXTURE.

SERVES FOUR

INGREDIENTS
- 500g/1¼lb leg of pork
- 1 large leek
- 2 large sheets tofu (bean curd) skin
- 1 egg, lightly beaten
- 5ml/1 tsp five-spice powder
- 15ml/1 tbsp light soy sauce
- 15ml/1 tbsp dark soy sauce
- 15ml/1 tbsp sesame oil
- 2.5ml/½ tsp black pepper
- oil for deep-frying
- lettuce leaves and chilli and garlic dip, to serve

COOK'S TIP
Tofu sheets are sold in Asian markets. It is important that the sheets are moistened before use so they can be rolled up without cracking.

1 With a heavy cleaver, chop the pork until it is fine and crumbly but not minced. Slice the leek very finely, discarding most of the green part.

2 Mix the pork with the leek, beaten egg, five-spice powder, sesame oil, soy sauces and pepper.

3 Spread out a tofu sheet on a flat surface and, with a damp cloth, lightly wipe it down to soften any crackly areas. Cut it into rectangles measuring 20 x 13cm/8 x 5in.

4 Place 30ml/2 tbsp of the pork mixture at one end of a rectangle, about 6cm/2½in from the edge. Roll the edge over the filling and pat in firmly. Roll once more and tuck in both sides before completing the rolling.

5 Repeat with the remaining wrappers and allow to rest for 10 minutes. Heat the oil and deep-fry the rolls for 4–5 minutes, until golden brown. Serve on a bed of lettuce with a sharp chilli and garlic dip.

Per portion Energy 207Kcal/872kJ; Protein 23.7g; Carbohydrate 19.7g, of which sugars 3.4g; Fat 4.2g, of which saturates 1g; Cholesterol 121mg; Calcium 241mg; Fibre 1.2g; Sodium 161mg.

VEGETABLES
AND SALADS

The tropical climate of Malaysia means that most vegetables are available all year round. Cool, colourful salads act as a foil for spicy snacks and curries, and often incorporate fresh fruits as well as crunchy vegetables. Exotic local vegetables such as water spinach and bamboo shoots are tossed into stir-fries and briefly cooked to retain all their colour and flavour, while Indian influences are revealed in slow-cooked vegetable curries.

MUSHROOMS <u>AND</u> BAMBOO SHOOTS <u>IN</u> YELLOW BEAN SAUCE

YELLOW BEAN SAUCE HAS A LOVELY, NUTTY TANG THAT BLENDS WELL WITH MOST INGREDIENTS. IT IS EASILY OBTAINED FROM ASIAN MARKETS OR MANY LARGE SUPERMARKETS. THE MUSHROOMS CAN BE CHINESE DRIED CEPS, FRESH SHIITAKE OR FIELD MUSHROOMS, OR SEVERAL DIFFERENT TYPES.

SERVES FOUR

INGREDIENTS

   150g/5oz mushrooms, any type,
     soaked until soft if dried
   150g/5oz canned bamboo shoots
   30ml/2 tbsp vegetable oil
   2 spring onions (scallions), chopped
   30g/2 tbsp yellow bean sauce
   5ml/1 tsp sugar
   175ml/6 fl oz/¾ cup water
   5ml/1 tsp cornflour (cornstarch),
     blended with a little water
   30ml/2 tbsp sesame oil

1 Cut each mushroom in half. Drain the bamboo shoots and rinse under cold running water, then drain again.

2 Heat the oil in a wok or large, heavy pan and fry the spring onions for 1 minute. Add the yellow bean sauce. Fry for 1 minute, then add the mushrooms and sliced bamboo shoots. Stir-fry over a high heat for about 2 minutes.

3 Add the sugar, water and cornflour blended with a little water. This will thicken the sauce very quickly. Stir for another minute.

4 Add the sesame oil, stir rapidly for 1 minute more and serve at once.

Per portion Energy 83Kcal/346kJ; Protein 2.4g; Carbohydrate 5.3g, of which sugars 2.4g; Fat 6g, of which saturates 0.7g; Cholesterol 0mg; Calcium 18mg; Fibre 1.5g; Sodium 34mg.

NONYA CABBAGE IN COCONUT MILK WITH GINGER AND CHILLI

IN MELAKA AND JOHOR, WHERE THE CUISINE IS DOMINATED BY THE CHINESE, MALAYS AND PERANAKANS, NONYA CUISINE FLOURISHES. WITH GOOD AGRICULTURAL GROUND, THERE IS AN ABUNDANCE OF VEGETABLES WHICH, IN THIS PART OF MALAYSIA, ARE COOKED IN COCONUT MILK.

SERVES FOUR

INGREDIENTS
  4 shallots, chopped
  2 garlic cloves, chopped
  1 lemon grass stalk, trimmed
    and chopped
  25g/1oz fresh root ginger, peeled
    and chopped
  2 red chillies, seeded and chopped
  5ml/1 tsp shrimp paste
  5ml/1 tsp turmeric powder
  5ml/1 tsp palm sugar (jaggery)
  15ml/1 tbsp sesame or groundnut
    (peanut) oil
  400ml/14fl oz/1⅔ cups coconut milk
  450g/1lb Chinese leaves (Chinese
    cabbage) or kale, cut into thick
    ribbons, or pak choi (bok choy),
    separated into leaves, or a mixture
    of the two
  salt and ground black pepper

VARIATION
To make a one-pot vegetable dish,
include a mixture of vegetables such as
string beans, carrots and leeks. You
could also add toasted peanuts or
cashews for protein and crunch.

1 First prepare the paste. Using a mortar and pestle or food processor, grind the shallots, garlic, lemon grass, ginger and chillies. Beat in the shrimp paste, turmeric and sugar.

2 Heat the oil in a wok or heavy pan, and stir in the spice paste. Cook, stirring continuously until the fragrances are released and the paste is beginning to colour.

3 Slowly pour in the coconut milk, mixing well, and bring the mixture to the boil. Simmer it to allow it to thicken into a creamy sauce.

4 Drop in the cabbage leaves, coating them in the coconut milk, and cook for a minute or two until the leaves have wilted. Season to taste and serve immediately in a warmed dish.

Per Portion Energy 112Kcal/469kJ; Protein 2.1g; Carbohydrate 13g, of which sugars 12.6g; Fat 6.1g, of which saturates 1g; Cholesterol 0mg; Calcium 89mg; Fibre 2.6g; Sodium 119mg.

STIR-FRIED BEANS WITH CHILLI SAUCE

YOU CAN USE YARD-LONG BEANS, FRENCH (GREEN) BEANS OR EVEN MANGETOUTS (SNOW PEAS) FOR THIS NUTRITIOUS VEGETARIAN DISH, AND ADJUST THE AMOUNT OF CHILLI SAUCE TO YOUR OWN TASTE. AS WITH MOST STIR-FRIED VEGETABLE DISHES, IT IS ALWAYS BETTER TO BLANCH THE VEGETABLES BEFORE FRYING SO THAT THEY TAKE UP THE SEASONINGS EFFECTIVELY AND COOK QUICKLY.

SERVES FOUR

INGREDIENTS
    400g/14oz yard-long beans
    30ml/2 tbsp oil
    2 garlic cloves, crushed
    5ml/1 tsp sugar
    30ml/2 tbsp chilli sauce, or amount
      to taste
    100ml/3½fl oz/scant ½ cup water

1 Trim the beans and cut them into 7.5cm/3in lengths.

2 Fill a pan with water and bring to the boil and blanch the beans for 2 minutes, then drain.

3 Heat the oil in a wok or heavy pan, add the garlic and fry until golden brown. Add the sugar and chilli sauce. Stir for 30 seconds then add the blanched beans. Stir rapidly for 2–3 minutes.

4 Add the water and bring quickly to the boil. Cook, stirring, until the beans are nearly dry. Serve hot with rice.

Per portion Energy 86Kcal/356kJ; Protein 2g; Carbohydrate 6.4g, of which sugars 5.4g; Fat 6g, of which saturates 0.8g; Cholesterol 0mg; Calcium 38mg; Fibre 2.3g; Sodium 122mg.

BRINJALS IN PEPPER GRAVY

This was originally a classic Nonya dish called kuah lada, calling for brinjal (aubergine), salt fish and meat in a hearty, peppery tamarind stock. This is a modified vegetarian version but it tastes just as good. In Malaysia, the local variety of aubergine is long and thin and ranges in colour from white to green, yellow or purple.

SERVES FOUR

INGREDIENTS
45ml/3 tbsp vegetable oil
1 large aubergine (eggplant)
500ml/17fl oz/generous 2 cups
  water
30ml/2 tbsp tamarind concentrate
2 stalks lemon grass, trimmed to
  7.5cm/3in of the root end, bruised
5ml/1 tsp salt
For the spice paste
3 red chillies, seeded and chopped
5 candlenuts
3 garlic cloves, chopped
8 shallots, chopped
15ml/1 tbsp black peppercorns
15g/½oz galangal, chopped
15g/½oz fresh turmeric, chopped

1 Grind all the ingredients for the spice paste together until fine, using a mortar and pestle or a food processor. Heat the oil in a pan and fry this spice paste for about 2 minutes, then stir in the water and tamarind concentrate. Bring to the boil before adding the lemon grass and salt. Turn the heat down slightly.

2 Leave the stock to simmer for 3 minutes while you slice the aubergine in half lengthways and cut it into half moon shapes about 2cm/¾in thick.

3 Add the aubergine to the stock and simmer for 15 minutes until soft. Adjust the seasoning and serve hot with rice.

Per portion Energy 122Kcal/506kJ; Protein 2.3g; Carbohydrate 8.5g, of which sugars 5.8g; Fat 9.1g, of which saturates 1.1g; Cholesterol 0mg; Calcium 35mg; Fibre 2.6g; Sodium 6mg.

STIR-FRIED SPICY AUBERGINE

THIS DISH IS BELIEVED TO HAVE COME FROM THE CHINESE PROVINCE OF HUPEI OR HUNAN, WHERE THE SAUCE USED HERE, CALLED DOU BANJIANG, IS VERY POPULAR. IT IS A BEAN PASTE INFUSED WITH SICHUAN PEPPERCORNS AND CHILLIES. AS IT IS A PUNGENT SAUCE, IT NEEDS TO BE TEMPERED WITH A LITTLE SUGAR TO STRIKE A YIN-YANG BALANCE. DOU BANJIANG, WHICH IS COMMONLY CALLED CHILLI BEAN SAUCE, IS SOLD IN EVERY CHINESE STORE, BUT YOU CAN EASILY MAKE YOUR OWN.

SERVES FOUR

INGREDIENTS
  2 large aubergines (eggplants)
  30ml/2 tbsp vegetable oil
  2 garlic cloves, crushed
  30ml/2 tbsp dou banjiang
  200ml/7fl oz/scant 1 cup water
  30ml/2 tbsp sesame oil
  5ml/1 tsp sugar

COOK'S TIP
To quickly make your own dou banjiang, or chilli bean sauce, blend 60ml/ 4 tbsp yellow bean sauce with 15ml/ 1 tbsp chilli sauce, 5ml/1 tsp ground Sichuan peppercorns and 30ml/2 tbsp sesame oil. This makes four times the quantity needed for this spicy aubergine dish. Store the sauce in a screw-top jar in the refrigerator.

1 Slice the aubergines in quarters lengthways then cut them across the grain into small chunks.

2 Bring a large pan of water to the boil and blanch the aubergines for 3 minutes, then drain thoroughly. This will loosen the cottony texture of the flesh to help it absorb the seasonings better.

3 Heat the oil and fry the garlic for 2 minutes. Add the dou banjiang and cook rapidly for 1 minute, stirring.

4 Add the aubergines and stir-fry for 2 minutes. Add the water and bring to a fast boil. Because they have been blanched, the aubergines will absorb the liquid more easily, hastening the cooking time. Simmer for about 4 minutes until the sauce has started to thickened a little.

5 Add the sesame oil and stir for 30 seconds. Season with sugar to taste, and serve the dish piping hot with rice or noodles.

Per portion Energy 121kcal/501kJ; Protein 1g; Carbohydrate 3.9g, of which sugars 3.4g; Fat 11.6g, of which saturates 1.6g; Cholesterol 0mg; Calcium 12mg; Fibre 2g; Sodium 73mg.

SARAWAK AUBERGINES WITH LEMON GRASS

THIS IS A GREAT WAY TO SERVE ANY AUBERGINE AVAILABLE. IF YOU CAN, TRY THE ROUND, ORANGE AUBERGINES GROWN BY DAYAK FARMERS, WHICH ARE PRETTY AND DELICATE IN FLAVOUR, AND PARTICULARLY TASTY COOKED IN COCONUT MILK WITH LOTS OF CHILLIES, GINGER AND LEMON GRASS. THE DAYAKS SERVE THIS DISH WITH THEIR LOCAL STAPLE, SAGO PORRIDGE, AND A HANDFUL OF FRESH CHILLIES FOR EXTRA FIRE, BUT IT IS DELICIOUS WITH PLAIN RICE OR CHUNKS OF CRUSTY BREAD.

SERVES FOUR

INGREDIENTS

15ml/1 tbsp ground turmeric
5ml/1 tsp chilli powder
3 slender orange aubergines
    (eggplants) or 8 baby aubergines,
    cut in wedges
45ml/3 tbsp vegetable or groundnut
    (peanut) oil
2 lemon grass stalks, trimmed,
    halved and bruised
600ml/1 pint/2½ cups
    coconut milk
salt and ground black pepper
a small bunch fresh coriander
    (cilantro), roughly chopped,
    to garnish
jasmine or coconut rice and
    2 green chillies, seeded and
    quartered lengthways (optional),
    to serve

For the spice paste

4–6 dried red chillies, soaked in
    warm water until soft, squeezed dry
    and seeded
4 garlic cloves, chopped
4 shallots, chopped
25g/1oz fresh root ginger, peeled
    and chopped
2 lemon grass stalks, trimmed
    and chopped
30ml/2 tbsp dried shrimp,
    re-hydrated in warm water
    and drained
5ml/1 tsp shrimp paste

1 First make the spice paste. Using a mortar and pestle or food processor, grind the chillies, garlic, shallots, ginger and lemon grass to a coarse paste. Grind in the dried shrimp and beat in the shrimp paste.

2 Mix the turmeric and chilli powder together. Rub the mixture all over the aubergine wedges.

COOK'S TIP

If you cannot find the orange aubergines used in this recipe, small purple ones can be substituted.

3 Heat the oil in a wok or heavy pan. Stir in the spice paste and lemon grass. Add the aubergine wedges, and cook until lightly browned. Pour in the coconut milk, stir well, and bubble it up to thicken.

4 Reduce the heat and cook gently for 15–20 minutes until the aubergine is tender but not mushy. Season with salt and pepper to taste. Sprinkle the coriander over the top and serve straight from the wok with the extra chillies to munch on, if you like. Serve with jasmine or coconut rice.

Per Portion Energy 154Kcal/644kJ; Protein 6.2g; Carbohydrate 11.9g, of which sugars 11g; Fat 9.5g, of which saturates 1.4g; Cholesterol 38mg; Calcium 175mg; Fibre 3g; Sodium 497mg.

ROASTED VEGETABLES <u>WITH</u> PEANUT SAUCE

Served as a vegetable side dish or as a main course, a selection of blanched, fried, grilled or roasted vegetables in a peanut sauce, enhanced by the usual chillies, soy sauce and other flavourings, is a great favourite throughout South-east Asia, especially with the Malays and Peranakans, who often eat it as a snack with bread.

SERVES FOUR

INGREDIENTS

   1 long, slender aubergine (eggplant), partially peeled and cut into long strips
   2 courgettes (zucchini), partially peeled and cut into long strips
   1 thick, long sweet potato, cut into long strips
   2 leeks, trimmed, halved widthways and lengthways
   2 garlic cloves, chopped
   25g/1oz fresh root ginger, peeled and chopped
   60ml/4 tbsp vegetable or groundnut (peanut) oil
   salt
   30ml/3 tbsp roasted peanuts, coarsely ground, to garnish
   fresh crusty bread, to serve
For the sauce
   4 garlic cloves, chopped
   2–3 red chillies, seeded and chopped
   5ml/1 tsp shrimp paste
   115g/4oz/1 cup roasted peanuts, crushed
   15–30ml/1–2 tbsp dark soy sauce
   juice of 1 lime
   5–10ml/1–2 tsp Chinese rice vinegar
   10ml/2 tsp palm sugar (jaggery) or clear honey
   salt and ground black pepper

COOK'S TIP
Aim to cut all the vegetables to a similar size and shape, so that they cook in roughly the same time. Long thin strips look good and give lots of sharp edges that will draw in the heat and brown and crisp appetizingly while the centres are still deliciously soft. The final peanut garnish adds extra crunch: the nuts should not be ground too fine.

1 Preheat the oven to 200°C/400°F/Gas 6. Arrange the vegetables in a shallow oven dish. Using a mortar and pestle or food processor, grind the garlic and ginger to a paste, and smear it evenly over the vegetables. Sprinkle with a little salt and pour over the oil.

2 Place the dish in the oven for about 45 minutes, until the vegetables are tender and slightly browned – toss them in the oil halfway through cooking.

3 Using a mortar and pestle or food processor, grind the garlic and chillies to a paste then beat in the other ingredients, with salt and pepper to taste. Blend with water to pouring (half-and-half) cream consistency.

4 Arrange the vegetables on a serving dish and drizzle the sauce over them. Sprinkle the ground peanuts over the top and serve warm with crusty bread.

Per Portion Energy 361Kcal/1502kJ; Protein 11.9g; Carbohydrate 22.7g, of which sugars 11.1g; Fat 25.4g, of which saturates 4.1g; Cholesterol 0mg; Calcium 76mg; Fibre 6.9g; Sodium 292mg.

GADO-GADO

THIS CLASSIC MIXED SALAD IS OF INDONESIAN ORIGIN, BUT IT IS ALSO VERY POPULAR IN MALAYSIA. IT IS DISTINGUISHED FROM OTHER SALADS BY THE CRUNCHY PEANUT AND COCONUT SAUCE SERVED WITH IT. THIS SALAD MAKES A PERFECT ACCOMPANIMENT TO A VARIETY OF SPICY DISHES AND CURRIES WITH ITS CLEAN TASTE AND BRIGHT, JEWEL-LIKE COLOURS.

SERVES SIX

INGREDIENTS
  ½ cucumber
  2 pears (not too ripe) or 175g/
    6oz wedge of yam bean
  1–2 eating apples
  juice of ½ lemon
  mixed salad leaves
  6 small tomatoes, cut in wedges
  3 slices fresh pineapple, cored and
    cut in wedges
  3 eggs, hard-boiled and shelled
  175g/6oz egg noodles, cooked,
    cooled and chopped
  deep-fried onions, to garnish
For the peanut sauce
  2–4 fresh red chillies, seeded
    and ground, or 15ml/
    1 tbsp chilli sambal
  300ml/½ pint/1¼ cups coconut milk
  350g/12oz/1¼ cups crunchy
    peanut butter

15ml/1 tbsp dark soy sauce or dark
  brown sugar
5ml/1 tsp tamarind pulp, soaked in
  45ml/3 tbsp warm water
coarsely crushed peanuts
salt

1 To make the peanut sauce, put the ground chillies or chilli sambal in a pan. Pour in the coconut milk, then stir in the peanut butter. Heat gently, stirring, until well blended.

2 Simmer gently until the sauce thickens, then stir in the soy sauce or sugar. Strain in the tamarind liquid, add salt to taste and stir well. Spoon into a bowl and sprinkle with a few coarsely crushed peanuts.

3 To make the salad, core the cucumber and peel the pears or yam bean. Cut them into matchsticks. Finely shred the apples and sprinkle them with the lemon juice.

4 Spread a bed of lettuce leaves on a flat platter or a section of banana leaf, then pile the prepared fruit and vegetables on top.

5 Add the sliced or quartered hard-boiled eggs, the chopped noodles and the deep-fried onions. Serve at once, with the sauce.

COOK'S TIP
Quail's eggs can be used instead of normal eggs and look very attractive in this dish. Hard boil for 3 minutes and halve or leave whole.

Per portion Energy 490Kcal/2043kJ; Protein18.9g; Carbohydrate 28.5g, of which sugars 21g; Fat 34.3g, of which saturates 8.6g; Cholesterol 116mg; Calcium 80mg; Fibre 6.2g; Sodium 493mg.

SPICY KANGKUNG <u>WITH</u> DRIED SHRIMP

KANGKUNG IS THE MALAY NAME FOR WATER SPINACH, OR MORNING GLORY, WHICH IS A WONDERFUL GREEN VEGETABLE WITH SPEAR-SHAPED LEAVES. THE VERSATILITY OF WATER SPINACH IS MUCH APPRECIATED THROUGHOUT SOUTH-EAST ASIA, WHERE IT IS USED IN SOUPS, FILLINGS AND BRAISED DISHES, OR SIMPLY STIR-FRIED ON ITS OWN. THIS DISH SERVES TWO AS A MAIN DISH OR FOUR AS A SIDE DISH.

SERVES TWO TO FOUR

INGREDIENTS
    4 garlic cloves, chopped
    25g/1oz fresh root ginger, peeled
      and chopped
    2 red chillies, seeded and chopped
    30ml/2 tbsp dried shrimp, soaked in
      warm water to soften and drained
    5ml/1 tsp shrimp paste
    30ml/2 tbsp vegetable or groundnut
      (peanut) oil
    7.5ml/1½1/2 tsp palm sugar (jaggery)
    15–30ml/1–2 tbsp light soy sauce
    500g/1¼lb fresh kangkung or
      water spinach leaves, washed
      and trimmed
    salt and ground black pepper
    1 red chilli, seeded and sliced,
      to garnish

1 Using a mortar and pestle or food processor, grind the garlic, ginger and chillies to a smooth paste. Add the dried shrimp and grind them to a paste. Beat in the shrimp paste and bind with a little of the oil.

2 Heat the rest of the oil in a wok or heavy pan. Stir in the spicy shrimp paste and cook over a low heat for 2–3 minutes until it is fragrant and beginning to colour. Stir in the sugar and soy sauce until well mixed.

3 Add the kangkung, tossing it around the pan so that all the leaves are coated in the spicy juices.

4 Cover with the lid for a few minutes to let the leaves wilt in the steam, then remove it and toss them around once more. Season to taste with salt and pepper, scatter the slices of red chilli over the top and serve immediately.

COOK'S TIP
Bundles of water spinach are sold in Chinese markets, but if it is not available you could replace it with ordinary garden spinach to make this dish. Serve it as a snack with bread and sliced chillies or as a side dish to accompany grilled or fried meats.

Per Portion Energy 107Kcal/441kJ; Protein 7.7g; Carbohydrate 4g, of which sugars 3.8g; Fat 6.7g, of which saturates 0.8g; Cholesterol 38mg; Calcium 304mg; Fibre 2.6g; Sodium 500mg.

ULAM VEGETABLES

THE TERM ULAM *REFERS TO THE PREPARATION OF FRESH VEGETABLES TO BE EATEN RAW WITH SPICES, A THROWBACK TO THE DIETARY HABITS OF MALAYSIAN JUNGLE DWELLERS, WHO ATE WITH THEIR FINGERS. THIS METHOD EVOLVED INTO THE MAINSTREAM MALAY STYLE OF EATING, AND ENTERED THE NONYA CULINARY REALM. ULAM IS ALWAYS SERVED COLD BUT CAN BE EATEN WITH WARM RICE.*

SERVES FOUR

INGREDIENTS
- 130g/4½oz long (snake) beans
- 1 cucumber
- 130g/4½oz cabbage
- 2 stalks lemon grass
- 2 red chillies
- 30ml/2 tbsp vegetable oil
- small bunch of sweet basil
- 5m/1 tsp salt
- 5ml/1 tsp sugar
- 30ml/2 tbsp lime juice
- 500g/1¼lb cooked rice, cold or warm

For the spice paste
- 30ml/2 tbsp dried shrimp
- 3 red chillies
- 15ml/1 tbsp shrimp paste
- 3 garlic cloves, chopped
- 4 shallots, chopped

1 Cut the long beans into small dice. Peel and seed the cucumber and cut it and the cabbage into similar-sized dice. Finely slice 5cm/2in of the root end of the lemon grass stalks and the chillies.

2 Grind together all the ingredients for the spice paste until fine. Heat the oil in a small pan and fry the paste for 3 minutes, until fragrant.

3 Put the prepared vegetables in a large bowl. Toss with the cooked rice and fried spices and add the salt, sugar and lime juice.

4 For an authentically rustic touch, serve the vegetable mixture on a banana leaf and get everyone to eat it with their fingers. Provide finger bowls, with a squeeze of lemon.

Per portion Energy 287Kcal/1211kJ; Protein 12g; Carbohydrate 45.1g, of which sugars 4.3g; Fat 7.8g, of which saturates 1.1g; Cholesterol 57mg; Calcium 197mg; Fibre 2.3g; Sodium 984mg.

CHINESE CHIVES WITH TOFU STIR-FRY

THESE CHIVES, ALSO KNOWN AS GARLIC CHIVES, ARE DIFFERENT FROM THE VARIETY USED AS A HERB IN THE WEST, BEING THICKER AND WITH A MORE PRONOUNCED AROMA. IN TRADITIONAL CHINESE MEDICINE THEY ARE VALUED FOR THEIR BLOOD-PURIFYING PROPERTIES AND ARE PURPORTED TO ALLEVIATE IMPOTENCE. THE TOFU REQUIRED FOR THIS DISH IS THE FIRM VARIETY.

SERVES FOUR

INGREDIENTS

- 275g/10oz Chinese chives
- 8 pieces of firm tofu (bean curd), 7.5cm/3in square and 4cm/1½in thick
- 30ml/2 tbsp vegetable oil
- 2 garlic cloves, crushed
- 30ml/2 tbsp light soy sauce
- 90ml/3 fl oz/¼ cup water

COOK'S TIP

Chinese or garlic chives are now widely available in supermarkets as well as in Asian markets. Both the leaves and the flower stems can be used.

1 Cut the chives into 7.5cm/3in lengths, wash and drain. Remove any that are tired-looking.

2 Cut each tofu cake into four. Heat the oil and fry them lightly until just brown.

3 Push the tofu aside and fry the garlic until light brown, then add the chives.

4 Stir-fry rapidly over high heat for 2 minutes. Add the soy sauce and water and stir for 2 minutes. Serve hot.

Per portion Energy 125Kcal/516kJ; Protein 8.2g; Carbohydrate 2.3g, of which sugars 1.8g; Fat 9.2g, of which saturates 1.1g; Cholesterol 0mg; Calcium 501mg; Fibre 1.5g; Sodium 633mg.

KERABU

KELANTAN IN THE NORTH OF MALAYSIA IS WELL KNOWN FOR ITS RICH TRADITIONAL MALAY CUISINE, PARTICULARLY NASI KERABU, THE FAMOUS BLUE RICE DISH, AND THIS LIVELY BEANSPROUT SALAD IS ALWAYS SERVED WITH IT. IN THE KOTA BHARU MARKETS, UP NEAR THE THAI BORDER, THE BLUE RICE IS WRAPPED IN A BANANA LEAF WITH KERABU AND EATEN AS A SNACK.

SERVES FOUR

INGREDIENTS

115g/4oz fresh coconut, grated
30ml/2 tbsp dried prawns (shrimp), soaked in warm water until soft
225g/8oz beansprouts, rinsed and drained
1 small cucumber, peeled, seeded and cut into julienne strips
2–3 spring onions (scallions), trimmed, cut into 2.5cm/1in pieces and halved lengthways
a handful of young, tender mangetouts (snow peas), halved diagonally
a handful of green beans, halved lengthways
a handful of fresh chives, chopped into 2.5cm/1in pieces
a handful of fresh mint leaves, finely chopped
2–3 red chillies, seeded and sliced finely lengthways
juice of 2 limes
10ml/2 tsp sugar
salt and ground black pepper

1 Dry-roast the coconut in a heavy pan until it is lightly browned and emits a nutty aroma. Using a mortar and pestle or a food processor, grind the roasted coconut to a coarse powder. Drain the soaked dried prawns and grind them coarsely too.

2 Put the vegetables, herbs and chillies into a bowl. Mix the lime juice with the sugar and pour it over the salad. Season with salt and pepper. Scatter the ground coconut and dried prawns over the salad, and toss well until thoroughly mixed.

Per Portion Energy 230Kcal/947kJ; Protein 12.6g; Carbohydrate 15.9g, of which sugars 13.9g; Fat 12.9g, of which saturates 10.2g; Cholesterol 0mg; Calcium 151mg; Fibre 7.8g; Sodium 24mg.

KAI LAN <small>WITH</small> KING PRAWNS

THIS ASIAN VEGETABLE COMES FROM THE SAME FAMILY AS TENDERSTEM BROCCOLI, AND IT IS A FAVOURITE AMONG THE CHINESE IN MALAYSIA. THE LEAVES ARE DARK GREEN AND THE THICK STALKS HAVE A NICE CRUNCH. THE CLASSIC CONDIMENT TO SERVE WITH THIS IS OYSTER SAUCE, WHICH IS A COMPLETE SEASONING, OBVIATING THE NEED TO ADD ANYTHING ELSE.

SERVES TWO

INGREDIENTS
- 200g/7oz kai lan
- 200g/7oz king or tiger prawns (jumbo shrimp)
- 2 garlic cloves, crushed
- 30ml/2 tbsp oil
- 30g/2 tbsp oyster sauce
- ½ tsp ground black pepper
- 90ml/3fl oz/¼ cup water

1 Trim off the hard ends of the kai lan stalks and slice into diagonal pieces about 7.5cm/3in long. Wash and dry.

2 Shell the prawns, wash and pat dry. Remove the dark veins by making a slit down the back of each prawn.

3 Heat the oil in a wok or large, heavy pan until it is smoking and throw in the kai lan. Stir-fry for 2 minutes, then add the prawns.

COOK'S TIP
A good splash of Chinese wine adds a lovely flavour: add this at any time.

4 Continue to stir-fry for 2 minutes while adding oyster sauce, pepper and water.

5 When the leaves wilt a little, the vegetables are done. Serve at once.

Per portion Energy 225Kcal/939kJ; Protein 22.3g; Carbohydrate 6.1g, of which sugars 5.7g; Fat 12.5g, of which saturates 1.6g; Cholesterol 195mg; Calcium 137mg; Fibre 2.8g; Sodium 443mg.

FRIED TOFU SALAD <u>WITH</u> A TANGY SAUCE

A GREAT FAVOURITE AT THE HAWKER STALLS, FRIED TOFU CAN EITHER BE STUFFED WITH BEANSPROUTS AND CUCUMBER AND THEN DRIZZLED WITH A SAUCE, OR ARRANGED AS A SALAD ON A PLATE. EITHER WAY, TAHU GORENG, AS THIS SALAD IS KNOWN, IS TANGY AND REFRESHING, AN IDEAL ACCOMPANIMENT TO GRILLED MEATS AND STIR-FRIED NOODLES. THE MALAYS, PERANAKANS AND EURASIANS ALL ENJOY THIS DISH, SO THE SAUCE VARIES FROM STALL TO STALL ACCORDING TO TASTE.

SERVES FOUR

INGREDIENTS
  vegetable oil, for deep-frying
  450g/1lb firm tofu (bean curd),
    rinsed, patted dry and cut into thick
    rectangular slices
  1 small cucumber, partially peeled in
    strips, seeded and shredded
  2 spring onions (scallions), trimmed,
    halved and shredded
  2 handfuls of fresh beansprouts
    rinsed and drained
  fresh coriander (cilantro) leaves,
    to garnish
For the sauce
  30ml/2 tbsp tamarind pulp, soaked
    in water until soft
  15ml/1 tbsp sesame or groundnut
    (peanut) oil
  4 shallots, finely chopped
  4 garlic cloves, finely chopped
  2 red chillies, seeded
  2.5ml/½ tsp shrimp paste
  115g/4oz/1 cup roasted
    peanuts, crushed
  30–45ml/2–3 tbsp kecap manis
  15ml/1 tbsp tomato ketchup

COOK'S TIP
If you cannot find kecap manis, which consists of soy sauce sweetened with palm sugar (jaggery), you could switch to ordinary soy sauce and increase the tomato ketchup to achieve a balance of sweet and sour in the sauce.

1 First make the sauce. Squeeze the tamarind pulp to soften it in the water, and then strain through a sieve. Measure 120ml/4fl oz/½ cup of the tamarind liquid. Discard the pulp.

2 Heat the oil in a wok and stir in the shallots, garlic and chillies, until fragrant. Stir in the shrimp paste and the peanuts. Add the kecap manis, ketchup and tamarind liquid and mix to a thick sauce. Leave to cool.

3 Heat enough oil for deep-frying in a wok or heavy pan. Slip in the blocks of tofu and fry until golden brown all over.

4 Remove the tofu from the pan and pat dry on kitchen paper. Cut each block into long, thin slices.

5 Arrange the tofu slices on a serving plate with the cucumber, spring onions and beansprouts.

6 Spoon the sauce over the tofu or serve it separately in a bowl. Garnish the salad with the coriander leaves.

Per Portion Energy 423Kcal/1749kJ; Protein 17.9g; Carbohydrate 7.8g, of which sugars 4.5g; Fat 35.8g, of which saturates 5.3g; Cholesterol 0mg; Calcium 607mg; Fibre 2.8g; Sodium 296mg.

CONDIMENTS

The essential condiments of South-east Asia add delicious flavours and textures to many dishes. Although they are often thought of as aromatic spicy dips or side dishes, they are in fact more than optional extras, often imparting the heat or flavour that really makes the meal. Wonderfully simple to prepare, the condiments in this chapter are exquisitely tasty and lift a feast of Malaysian dishes to memorably flavoursome heights.

SAMBAL BELACAN

THIS IS THE UBIQUITOUS CONDIMENT OF THE MALAYS AND PERANAKANS. AS THEY HAVE SUCH A PENCHANT FOR STRONG, FIERY TASTES, THIS PUNCHY CONDIMENT GRACES THEIR TABLES ON A DAILY BASIS. A LITTLE BOWLFUL SEEMS TO GO WITH EVERYTHING: CHUNKS OF BREAD, RICE, GRILLED FOODS AND STIR-FRIED VEGETABLES. THE PUNGENT SHRIMP PASTE, BELACAN, IS MADE FROM TINY SHRIMP MASHED TO A PASTE AND BURIED FOR SEVERAL MONTHS TO FERMENT.

SERVES FOUR

INGREDIENTS

    15ml/1 tbsp shrimp paste
    4 fresh red chillies, seeded (reserve
      the seeds)
    2 kaffir lime leaves, spines removed,
      and chopped
    2.5ml/½ tsp sugar
    1.5ml/¼ tsp salt
    juice of 1 lime
    1 lime, quartered, to serve

COOK'S TIP

The fermented shrimp paste, belacan, is available in Asian markets. If you cannot get hold of it, replace it with the more readily available Thai shrimp paste.

1 In a small, heavy pan, dry-roast the shrimp paste until it is aromatic and crumbly. Using a mortar and pestle or food processor, grind the roasted shrimp paste with the chillies to form a paste. Grind in half the chilli seeds and the lime leaves.

2 Add the sugar and salt, and stir in the rest of the chilli seeds. Moisten with the lime juice. Spoon the sambal into little dishes and serve with wedges of lime to squeeze over it.

Per Portion Energy 17Kcal/69kJ; Protein 2.8g; Carbohydrate 0.8g, of which sugars 0.8g; Fat 0.3g, of which saturates 0g; Cholesterol 19mg; Calcium 53mg; Fibre 0g; Sodium 312mg.

SAMBAL SERONDENG

A QUINTESSENTIAL DRESSING FOR CURRIES IN MALAYSIA, SERONDENG ORIGINATED IN INDONESIA, WHERE IT WAS EATEN WITH RIJSTAFEL, A MOUTHWATERING MELANGE OF DISHES BUILT AROUND RICE, WHOSE DUTCH NAME LITERALLY MEANS "RICE TABLE". THE PERANAKAN COMMUNITY IN MALAYSIA ADOPTED THIS IDEA FOR THEIR FESTIVE TOK PANJANG, OR "LONG TABLE", AND ALSO BORROWED THE RECIPE FOR SAMBAL SERONDENG, OF WHICH THERE ARE SEVERAL VERSIONS.

SERVES SIX TO EIGHT

INGREDIENTS
  2 stalks lemon grass
  5 shallots
  4 garlic cloves
  3 fresh red chillies, seeded
   (optional)
  50g/2oz tempeh (fermented soy
   bean cake)
  30ml/2 tbsp vegetable or groundnut
   (peanut) oil
  175g/6oz fresh coconut, grated or
   100g/3½oz desiccated (dry,
   unsweetened, shredded) coconut
  2.5ml/½ tsp salt
  2.5ml/½ tsp sugar

1 Trim the lemon grass stalks and slice the 7.5cm/3in at the root end into very thin rounds. Peel and slice the shallots and the garlic. Slice the chillies diagonally into thin pieces.

2 Cut the tempeh into small dice, and fry it in oil in a wok or heavy pan until light brown. Crush it coarsely.

3 Heat another wok without oil and dry fry the lemon grass, shallots, garlic and chillies until just sizzled. Add the coconut, and stir-fry with a to and fro motion until all the ingredients are golden brown.

4 Add the crushed tempeh, salt and sugar and fry, stirring, until well-mixed. Remove from the heat and leave to cool before storing in an air-tight container, if not serving immediately. Keep the serondeng in the refrigerator and eat within a week.

COOK'S TIPS
Serondeng is delicious sprinkled over dishes like beef rendang, coconut milk kormas and curries or over plain rice as a relish. Use freshly grated coconut for the best flavour as store-bought desiccated coconut is over-dehydrated. Good serondeng should be succulent and softly moist.

Per portion Energy 120Kcal/494kJ; Protein 1.7g; Carbohydrate 4.1g, of which sugars 3.3g; Fat 10.8g, of which saturates 7g; Cholesterol 0mg; Calcium 44mg; Fibre 2.2g; Sodium 128mg.

SOUR MANGO SAMBAL

ANOTHER MALAY FAVOURITE IS SAMBAL ASAM, SOUR SAMBAL, MADE WITH GREEN MANGO OR PAPAYA. IT IS SERVED IN SMALL QUANTITIES AS A RELISH TO ACCOMPANY FRIED FISH AND SHELLFISH, SPICY GRILLED FOODS AND FIERY CURRIES, BUT IT CAN ALSO BE SERVED ON ITS OWN AS A REFRESHING SNACK.

SERVES FOUR

INGREDIENTS
  5ml/1 tsp shrimp paste
  4 fresh red chillies, seeded
  7.5ml/1½ tsp salt
  5ml/1 tsp sugar
  1 green mango, peeled and shredded
  juice of ½ lime

1 In a small, heavy pan, dry-roast the shrimp paste over a low heat until it is aromatic and crumbly.

COOK'S TIP
Mangoes are widely available, but for this recipe you need an unripe fruit, in which the flesh is just starting to turn yellow.

2 Using a mortar and pestle or food processor, grind the chillies with the salt to form a paste. Add the shrimp paste and sugar and pound into the spicy paste. Toss in the shredded mango and moisten with the lime juice. Mix well and serve in little bowls.

Per Portion Energy 34Kcal/143kJ; Protein 1.7g; Carbohydrate 6.5g, of which sugars 6.4g; Fat 0.3g, of which saturates 0.1g; Cholesterol 6mg; Calcium 28mg; Fibre 1g; Sodium 794mg.

PINEAPPLE PICKLE

THIS SPICY SWEET-AND-SOUR PICKLE IS IDEAL TO SERVE WITH GRILLED FOODS OR AS A FRUITY ACCOMPANIMENT TO CURRIES OR VEGETABLE DISHES. MALAYS LIKE THEIR PICKLES HOT, BUT YOU CAN ADJUST THE AMOUNT OF CHILLI IN THIS RECIPE TO SUIT YOUR TASTE.

SERVES SIX TO EIGHT

INGREDIENTS

15ml/1 tbsp brown mustard seeds
2 dried chillies, soaked in water until soft, squeezed dry and seeded
15g/½oz fresh root ginger, peeled and chopped
1 garlic clove, chopped
5ml/1 tsp ground turmeric
200ml/7fl oz/scant 1 cup white wine vinegar or rice vinegar
15ml/1 tbsp palm sugar (jaggery)
1 ripe pineapple
salt

1 In a small, heavy pan, dry-roast the mustard seeds until they pop.

2 Using a mortar and pestle or food processor, grind the chillies, ginger and garlic to a paste. Stir in the mustard seeds and ground turmeric. Add the vinegar and sugar, stirring until the sugar has completely dissolved.

COOK'S TIP
Malays and Indians often serve a selection of condiments with every meal. The Malay sambal, the Nonya acar and myriad Indian pickles can all be interchanged with the food of these cultures.

3 Peel and core the pineapple and dice the flesh. Put the pineapple in a bowl and pour over the pickling sauce. Add salt to taste. The pickle will keep for 2–3 days in the refrigerator.

Per Portion Energy 56Kcal/238kJ; Protein 0.7g; Carbohydrate 12.5g, of which sugars 12.2g; Fat 0.2g, of which saturates 0g; Cholesterol 0mg; Calcium 20mg; Fibre 1.3g; Sodium 4mg.

LIME PICKLE

THIS INDIAN PICKLE IS POPULAR AMONG MALAYS, EURASIANS AND PERANAKANS, AS WELL AS THE INDIAN COMMUNITIES OF MALAYSIA. OFTEN SOLD IN JARS AT HAWKER STALLS, THE PICKLE IS EATEN MAINLY AS AN ACCOMPANIMENT TO FIERY CURRIES. COMMERCIAL VARIETIES OF THIS FAMOUS PICKLE ARE WIDELY AVAILABLE, BUT CANNOT COMPARE WITH THIS FRESHLY MADE VERSION.

SERVES EIGHT TO TEN

INGREDIENTS
- 8–10 limes
- 30ml/2 tbsp salt
- 150ml/5fl oz/⅔ cup sesame or groundnut (peanut) oil
- 10–15ml/2–3 tsp brown mustard seeds
- 3–4 garlic cloves, cut into thin sticks
- 25g/1oz fresh root ginger, peeled and cut into thin sticks
- 5ml/1 tsp coriander seeds
- 5ml/1 tsp cumin seeds
- 5ml/1 tsp fennel seeds
- 10ml/2 tsp ground turmeric
- 10ml/2 tsp hot chilli powder or paste
- a handful of fresh or dried curry leaves

1 Put the whole limes in a bowl. Cover with boiling water and leave to stand for 30 minutes. Drain and cut into quarters. Rub the lime pieces with salt and put them into a sealed sterilized jar. Leave the limes to cure in the salt for 1 week.

2 Heat the oil in a wok and stir in the mustard seeds. When they begin to pop, stir in the garlic, ginger, spices and curry leaves. Cook gently for a few minutes to flavour the oil, then stir in the lime pieces and the juices from the jar. Reduce the heat and simmer the pickle for about 45 minutes, stirring from time to time.

3 Pour the pickle into sterilized jars and store in a cool place for 1–2 months.

COOK'S TIP
This pickle is delicious served with grilled (broiled) or fried fish, and spicy stir-fried noodles. You can make it as fiery as you like by adding more or less chilli powder.

Per Portion Energy 96Kcal/395kJ; Protein 0.3g; Carbohydrate 0.9g, of which sugars 0.6g; Fat 10.1g, of which saturates 1.5g; Cholesterol 0mg; Calcium 25mg; Fibre 0.2g; Sodium 1185mg.

NONYA ACAR

THERE ARE NUMEROUS VERSIONS OF ACAR, *A PICKLE CREATED IN* NONYA *KITCHENS.* PENANG ACAR, ACAR KUNIN *AND* ACAR AWAK *ALL CONSIST OF A MEDLEY OF VEGETABLES THAT CAN BE SERVED AS A RELISH OR SIDE DISH. MORE ELABORATE THAN* MALAY *AND* INDIAN *PICKLES,* NONYA ACAR *RECIPES VARY FROM ONE HOUSEHOLD TO ANOTHER, SO YOU CAN EXPERIMENT WITH DIFFERENT VEGETABLES.*

SERVES SIX TO TEN

INGREDIENTS
- 450g/1lb carrots, peeled and cut into matchsticks
- 450g/1lb daikon (mooli or white radish), peeled and cut into matchsticks
- 2 small cucumbers, halved lengthways, seeded and cut into matchsticks
- 6 dried red chillies, soaked in warm water to soften, squeezed dry and seeded
- 6 garlic cloves, chopped
- 50g/2oz fresh root ginger, peeled and chopped
- 50g/2oz fresh turmeric, chopped
- 30ml/2 tbsp vegetable or groundnut (peanut) oil
- 6 shallots, sliced
- 2 lemon grass stalks, halved and bruised
- 45–60ml/3–4 tbsp rice or white wine vinegar
- 30ml/2 tbsp sugar
- 45ml/3 tbsp roasted peanuts
- 30ml/2 tbsp roasted sesame seeds
- salt

4 Season to taste with salt and put the vegetables into a large serving bowl. Leave the mixture to cool, then toss in the peanuts and sesame seeds. The pickle can be stored in a non-metallic container in the refrigerator, or a cool place, for 3–4 days.

1 Put the vegetables into a bowl, sprinkle with salt and set aside for about 15 minutes. Rinse the vegetables, drain and pat dry.

2 Using a mortar and pestle or a food processor, grind the chillies, garlic, ginger and turmeric together until they form a smooth paste.

3 Heat the oil in a wok. Stir in the shallots and lemon grass and fry until golden. Stir in the spice paste and fry until fragrant. Add the vegetables, tossing them around the wok to coat them in the spices. Add the vinegar and sugar and continue to cook the vegetables until they are tender, with just a little bite to them.

Per Portion Energy 96Kcal/398kJ; Protein 2.3g; Carbohydrate 9.6g, of which sugars 8.8g; Fat 5.6g, of which saturates 0.9g; Cholesterol 0mg; Calcium 52mg; Fibre 2.3g; Sodium 18mg.

LIME AND CHILLI DIP

*FOR THIS MALAY DIP, SAMBAL LIMAU, IT IS BEST TO USE CALAMANSI (ALSO KNOWN AS KESTURI)
LIMES, WHICH ARE INDIGENOUS TO SOUTH-EAST ASIA AND HAVE VERY THIN SKINS THAT CAN BE
GRATED TO ADD TO THE SAUCE. WEST INDIAN LIMES CAN BE USED PROVIDED YOU GRATE THE SKIN
VERY THINLY, OTHERWISE THE SAUCE WILL HAVE QUITE A BITTER EDGE. CALAMANSI OR KESTURI
LIMES ARE OCCASIONALLY AVAILABLE IN THAI AND FILIPINO MARKETS.*

SERVES FOUR TO SIX

INGREDIENTS
    6 calamansi limes
    4 red chillies
    2 garlic cloves
    2 spring onions (scallions)
    2 kaffir lime leaves
    15ml/1 tbsp fish sauce
    5ml/1 tsp sugar
    30ml/2 tbsp water

1 Finely grate the rind of one lime into a
bowl. Squeeze the juice from all the
limes into the bowl and, with a spoon,
scoop out the flesh. Discard the seeds.

2 Finely chop the chillies, garlic and
spring onions. Shred the lime leaves
finely. Mix these ingredients into the
lime juice and add the sugar, fish sauce
and water. Stir everything together.

3 Taste and adjust the proportions if
necessary, adding more water or lime
juice as needed. Serve the dip with fish
and chicken dishes or salads.

Per portion Energy 9Kcal/38kJ; Protein 0.6g; Carbohydrate 1.6g, of which sugars 1.3g; Fat 0.1g, of which saturates 0g; Cholesterol 0mg; Calcium 6mg; Fibre 0.1g; Sodium 179mg.

CHILLI, GARLIC AND GINGER SAUCE

REGARDED AS THE HOLY TRINITY OF HERBS, CHILLIES, GARLIC AND GINGER HAVE AN EXTRAORDINARY AFFINITY WHEN THEY ARE COMBINED IN THE CORRECT PROPORTIONS. FIRST, THE CHILLIES MUST BE ABSOLUTELY FRESH, RED, AND AS HOT AS TASTE DICTATES. THE GARLIC SHOULD BE FRESH AND PLUMP WITH NO WRINKLY SKINS. THE BEST GINGER ROOTS FOR THIS SAUCE ARE THE TENDER YOUNG STEMS, IDEALLY WITH SHORT PALE GREEN STALKS STILL ATTACHED TO THEM.

MAKES ABOUT 300ML/½ PINT/1½ CUPS

INGREDIENTS
   10 fresh red chillies
   10 cloves garlic
   50g/2oz fresh root ginger
   200ml/7fl oz/scant 1 cup rice
     wine vinegar
   2.5ml/½ tsp salt
   30ml/2 tbsp vegetable oil
   2 spring onions (scallions)
   2.5ml/½ tsp sugar

1 Wash the chillies and pat them dry. It is important that you do not introduce moisture into the sauce as it will encourage bacterial growth and the sauce will not keep well. Do not remove the seeds of the chillies in this case as the sauce is intended to give sweet, sharp fire to dishes. Chop roughly.

2 Peel the garlic and wipe dry with kitchen paper: do not wash it. Chop the flesh roughly.

3 With a sharp paring knife, peel or scrape off the thin outer skin of the ginger. If the roots you are using have any green stems attached, do not discard these. Roughly chop the ginger.

COOK'S TIP
When ready to eat, scoop out as much as is needed with a clean dry spoon and add more rice wine vinegar and sugar to the sauce to taste.

4 Place all three ingredients in a mortar and pestle or food processor and process until fine, but be careful not to reduce it to a purée consistency. To facilitate the grinding, add a spoonful or two of the vinegar.

5 Turn the mixture into a bowl and combine with the remaining vinegar and the salt. Heat the oil in a small pan or wok and add to the sauce. Finely chop the spring onions and mix them in well. Keep in a jar with a screw-top lid.

Per portion Energy 339Kcal/1405kJ; Protein 13.9g; Carbohydrate 18.1g, of which sugars 3.5g; Fat 23.9g, of which saturates 2.7g; Cholesterol 0mg; Calcium 100mg; Fibre 4.6g; Sodium 1070mg.

GINGER AND GARLIC SALT

THIS IS A CLASSIC DIP FOR CANTONESE DEEP-FRIED CHICKEN. IT IS VERY EASY TO MAKE. IF YOU CAN FIND COARSE-GRAINED SEA SALT, IT IS IDEAL FOR THIS MIXTURE, AS IT HAS A FULLER FLAVOUR AND AN APPETIZINGLY FLAKY TEXTURE, AS WELL AS A LOWER SODIUM CONTENT.

MAKES ENOUGH AS A DIP FOR 1 CHICKEN

INGREDIENTS

   50g/2oz fresh root ginger, peeled
   4 garlic cloves
   30ml/2 tbsp vegetable oil
   15ml/1 tbsp sesame oil
   2.5ml/½ tsp sugar
   5ml/1 tsp salt
   2.5ml/½ tsp freshly ground
     black pepper
   1 spring onion (scallion)

COOK'S TIP
If you don't have a microwave, heat the mixture in a small pan for 2 minutes.

1 Grate the ginger and finely chop the garlic. Blend in a small bowl and mix in the oils, sugar, salt and pepper. Microwave for 1 minute to cook the oil so the sauce will not have a raw taste.

2 Chop the spring onion very finely and stir it into the sauce. Leave the sauce to cool and store it in a jar with a screw top, in the refrigerator, if you are not using it immediately.

Per portion Energy 401Kcal/1650kJ; Protein 0.5g; Carbohydrate 0.8g, of which sugars 0.7g; Fat 44.1g, of which saturates 5.8g; Cholesterol 0mg; Calcium 27mg; Fibre 0.7g; Sodium 1996mg.

DRIED SHRIMP AND CHILLI CONDIMENT

LOOK FOR DRIED SHRIMPS THAT ARE LARGE, UNBROKEN AND A DULL PINKISH BROWN. THEY ARE MUCH EASIER TO PROCESS WHEN SOAKED BRIEFLY IN WARM WATER UNTIL JUST SOFT BUT NOT MUSHY. THAI AND LAOTIAN COOKS GRILL OR CHAR THEIR SPRING ONIONS TO IMPART A SMOKY FLAVOUR TO THIS SAUCE.

SERVES FOUR

INGREDIENTS
    2 spring onions (scallions)
    50g/2oz dried shrimps
    6 shallots
    4 garlic cloves
    30ml/2 tbsp water
    30ml/2 tbsp lime juice
    5ml/1 tsp sugar

1 Hold the spring onions by their green tops and run the white parts briefly over a gas flame until they are lightly charred and frizzled. Then trim and cut the spring onions into short lengths of approximately 2.5cm/1in.

2 Peel and slice the garlic and shallots. Grind them together with the spring onions in a mortar and pestle or a food processor to a coarse paste. Remove the paste to a bowl, then grind the soaked dried shrimps finely. Add them to the bowl and mix all the ingredients together thoroughly.

3 Add the lime juice, sugar and water and blend well.

Per portion Energy 59kcal/247kJ; Protein 8.1g; Carbohydrate 6g, of which sugars 4.1g; Fat 0.5g, of which saturates 0.1g; Cholesterol 63mg; Calcium 166mg; Fibre 1g; Sodium 543mg.

DESSERTS AND DRINKS

The abundant tropical fruit available at all times of year is often eaten at the end a meal, or as a refreshing snack during the day, or turned into cooling water ices or juices. The inhabitants of Malaysia also enjoy a variety of very sweet snacks, rich with palm sure or coconut cream and eggs, and fragrant with pandan and spices. Baked, fried or steamed, they are sold at the hawker stalls and eaten while still warm.

ROASTED COCONUT ICE CREAM

THE POPULARITY OF ICE CREAM IN MALAYSIA ENSURES THAT, IN THE CITIES AT LEAST, YOU WILL NOT HAVE TO SEARCH FOR VERY LONG BEFORE YOU FIND IT. ICE CREAM TRUCKS SET THEMSELVES UP AT BUSY STREET CORNERS, IN SHOPPING CENTRES AND ENTERTAINMENT PARKS, SELLING AN EXOTIC SELECTION, WITH FLAVOURS RANGING FROM FRUITY PASSION FRUIT, MANGO, SOUR PLUM AND DURIAN TO RICH AND CREAMY COCONUT, AVOCADO AND CORN.

SERVES FOUR TO SIX

INGREDIENTS

  115g/4oz fresh coconut, finely
    chopped in a food processor
  4 large (US extra large) egg yolks
  115g/4oz/generous ½ cup sugar
  900ml/1½ pints/3¾ cups coconut
    milk
  250ml/8fl oz/1 cup double
    (heavy) cream
  25ml/1½ tbsp rice flour, blended
    with 30ml/2 tbsp coconut milk
    or cream
  salt

1 Roast the coconut in a heavy frying pan over a medium heat until nicely browned and emitting a nutty aroma. Transfer to a plate and leave to cool.

2 In a bowl, whisk the egg yolks with the sugar until pale and creamy. In a heavy pan, heat the coconut milk with the cream and a generous pinch of salt to scalding point. Gradually pour the hot coconut milk into the egg yolk mixture, whisking vigorously at the same time to form a smooth custard. Strain the custard into a clean heavy pan and stir it gently over a low heat, until slightly thickened.

3 Beat the rice flour mixture into the custard until it coats the back of a wooden spoon. Pour the custard into a bowl or freezer-proof container and leave to cool.

4 Stir most of the roasted coconut (reserve a little for decorating) into the cooled custard and put it in the freezer until frozen, taking it out and stirring after about half an hour. Alternatively, churn in an ice cream maker according to the manufacturer's instructions.

5 To serve, sprinkle the ice cream with the reserved roasted coconut.

Per Portion Energy 448Kcal/1863kJ; Protein 4.1g; Carbohydrate 32.5g, of which sugars 29.1g; Fat 34.3g, of which saturates 21.9g; Cholesterol 192mg; Calcium 95mg; Fibre 1.8g; Sodium 191mg.

SWEET PURÉED AVOCADO

This sweet avocado snack is thought to have originated with the Dutch in Melaka, but now it is also served in Penang, where it is popular with the sweet-toothed Malays, Indians, Eurasians and, of course, tourists. It can be served as a thick purée or blended with coconut milk until it is the consistency of thick pouring cream. It can also be enjoyed as a sweet drink with a couple of ice cubes stirred in.

SERVES TWO

INGREDIENTS
    1 avocado, stoned (pitted)
    juice of ½ lime
    30ml/2 tbsp sweetened
      condensed milk
    30ml/2 tbsp coconut cream
    a pinch of salt
    fresh mint leaves, to decorate
    ½ lime, halved, to serve

1 Put the avocado flesh into a food processor and purée it with the lime juice. Add the condensed milk, coconut cream and salt and process until the mixture is smooth and creamy.

2 Spoon into individual bowls or glasses and chill over ice. Decorate with a few mint leaves and serve with lime wedges to squeeze over it.

VARIATION
This recipe works equally well with other soft-fleshed fruit, such as bananas, mango and papaya.

Per Portion Energy 243Kcal/1006kJ; Protein 3.2g; Carbohydrate 10.3g, of which sugars 9.2g; Fat 21.2g, of which saturates 8.5g; Cholesterol 5mg; Calcium 54mg; Fibre 2.6g; Sodium 421mg.

SAGO PUDDING WITH PALM SUGAR SYRUP

IN SABAH AND SARAWAK, SAGO IS THE MAIN STAPLE AND THE SAGO PALM IS KNOWN AS THE "TREE OF A THOUSAND USES", AS IT SUPPLIES NOT ONLY FOOD BUT BUILDING AND CRAFT MATERIALS AND MEDICINE. SAGO PEARLS ARE USED IN BOTH SAVOURY AND SWEET DISHES, SUCH AS THIS ONE. THIS SWEET PUDDING, SAGU GULA MELAKA, IS ALSO ENJOYED IN MANY MALAY HOMES THROUGHOUT THE PENINSULA. THE INTENSE SWEETNESS OF THE PALM SUGAR SYRUP IS AN ESSENTIAL ACCOMPANIMENT.

3 Drain the sago through a sieve (strainer) and rinse under cold running water.

4 Reserve the pandan leaf. Put the sago in a bowl and stir in 15–30ml/1–2 tbsp of the coconut milk with a pinch of salt.

5 Spoon the sago into a lightly greased mould, or four individual moulds, packing it down gently, and leave at room temperature to set.

6 Meanwhile, make the syrup. Put the water and palm sugar into a heavy pan and stir over a high heat until the sugar dissolves.

7 Bring to the boil and boil for 2 minutes. Drop in the reserved pandan leaf, reduce the heat, and simmer for 10 minutes, stirring from time to time.

8 Beat the rest of the coconut milk with a pinch of salt. Turn the mould, or moulds, upside down in a shallow bowl and slip them off the pudding.

9 Spoon the coconut milk over the top, allowing it to flow down the sides and form a pool in the dish.

10 Pour the hot syrup all over the pudding, allowing plenty for each person. Serve the dessert immediately, while the syrup is still hot.

SERVES FOUR

INGREDIENTS
1 pandan (screwpine) leaf, tied in a knot
250g/9oz pearl sago, picked over, washed and drained
400ml/14fl oz/1⅔ cups coconut milk, lightly beaten
salt
For the syrup
250ml/8fl oz/1 cup water
175g/6oz/¾ cup palm sugar (jaggery)

VARIATIONS
Alternatively, you could keep the sago hot in a steamer and heat up the coconut milk, so that the whole pudding is hot. If you cannot find pandan leaves, use a vanilla pod (bean) to flavour the pudding instead.

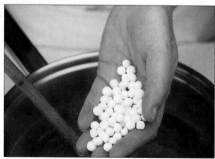

1 Bring a deep pan of water to the boil. Drop in the pandan leaf and let the sago pour into the water through the fingers of one hand, while you stir with a wooden spoon, to prevent the pearls from sticking.

2 Boil for 5 minutes, then remove from the heat, cover and leave the sago to steam for about 10 minutes – the sago pearls will go swollen and translucent.

Per Portion Energy 416Kcal/1777kJ; Protein 0.7g; Carbohydrate 109.4g, of which sugars 50.6g; Fat 0.4g, of which saturates 0.2g; Cholesterol 0mg; Calcium 59mg; Fibre 0.3g; Sodium 115mg.

EGG CUSTARD <small>IN</small> PUMPKIN

THIS UNUSUAL DESSERT HAS ARRIVED IN MALAYSIA FROM THAILAND, WHERE IT IS CALLED SANGKAYA FAKTONG AND IS TRADITIONALLY MADE WITH DUCK EGGS. MALAYSIAN COOKS HAVE ADOPTED THE IDEA WITH GUSTO, AND IT MAKES A SPECTACTULAR DESSERT FOR A PARTY. YOU DO NOT SPECIFICALLY HAVE TO USE EITHER PUMPKIN OR DUCK EGGS TO MAKE THIS RECIPE. ANY GOOD-LOOKING SQUASH CAN BE USED AS THE "BOWL" FOR THE CUSTARD, AND HENS' EGGS ARE PERFECTLY SATISFACTORY.

SERVES FOUR

INGREDIENTS
6 large (US extra large) eggs
250ml/8fl oz/1 cup coconut cream
150g/5oz palm sugar (jaggery)
1 pumpkin, about 20cm/8in
in diameter.

1 Grate the sugar. Beat the eggs lightly and whisk in the coconut cream and sugar. Cut off the top of the pumpkin and scoop out seeds and fibres.

2 Pour in the frothy custard mixture, cover with the pumpkin top and place the pumpkin in a steamer.

3 Cover the steamer and steam for 25 minutes until the custard is set. Allow to cool and cut into slices to serve, but do not eat the pumpkin skin.

COOK'S TIP
If you use only egg yolks (for this, increase the number to 8), the results will be even richer.

Per portion Energy 217Kcal/907kJ; Protein 4.6g; Carbohydrate 16.3g, of which sugars 15.7g; Fat 15.4g, of which saturates 11.9g; Cholesterol 71mg; Calcium 71mg; Fibre 1.3g; Sodium 88mg.

PUMPKIN, SWEET POTATO <u>AND</u> BANANA <u>IN</u> COCONUT MILK

THIS DISH OF SWEET VEGETABLES IS A POPULAR DESSERT IN THE JUNGLES AND FIELDS OF SARAWAK, SABAH AND THE RURAL AREAS OF THE MALAYSIAN PENINSULA, WITH RECIPES INCLUDING ALL KINDS OF DELICIOUS OF GOURDS SUCH AS YAM, BUTTERNUT SQUASH AND WINTER MELON.

SERVES FOUR TO SIX

INGREDIENTS
 900ml/1½ pints/3¾ cups
  coconut milk
 ½ small pumpkin, seeded and cut
  into bitesize cubes
 2 sweet potatoes, cut into
  bitesize pieces
 1 pandan (screwpine) leaf
 150g/5oz/¾ cup palm sugar (jaggery)
 2.5ml/½ tsp salt
 3 bananas, cut into thick
  diagonal slices

1 Bring the coconut milk to the boil in a heavy pan. Stir in the pumpkin, sweet potatoes and pandan leaf.

2 Continue to boil for 1 minute, then reduce the heat and simmer for about 15 minutes, until the pumpkin and sweet potato are tender but retain their shape well.

3 Using a slotted spoon, lift the pumpkin and sweet potato pieces out of the coconut milk and put them on a plate.

4 Add the sugar and salt to the coconut milk and stir until the sugar has dissolved. Bring the sweetened coconut milk to the boil, then reduce the heat and simmer for 5 minutes.

5 Add the bananas to the sweetened coconut milk and simmer for 4 minutes.

6 Put the pumpkin and sweet potato back into the pan and gently mix all the ingredients together.

7 Remove the pandan leaf and serve the dessert warm.

Per Portion Energy 249Kcal/1063kJ; Protein 2.6g; Carbohydrate 61.4g, of which sugars 51.7g; Fat 1g, of which saturates 0.5g; Cholesterol 0mg; Calcium 97mg; Fibre 2.8g; Sodium 187mg.

MALAYSIAN MASHED AND FRIED BANANA FRITTERS

A really memorable dish from rural Malaysia, though not to be confused with the Chinese dish. This recipe uses mashed bananas, which are thickened with rice flour and fried in spoonfuls until brown, then dipped in caster sugar. Any type of banana will do.

SERVES FOUR

INGREDIENTS
4 large bananas
130g/4½oz rice flour
1 egg, lightly beaten
oil for deep-frying
caster (superfine) sugar, for dusting

1 Peel the bananas and mash them with a fork to a pulp. Sift the rice flour over and blend with the banana mash. Beat in the egg to bind the mixture.

2 Heat the oil for deep-frying in a wok or large pan. Drop in a heaped tablespoonful of mash at a time until golden brown. Lift out with a slotted spoon and drain on kitchen paper.

3 Spread some caster sugar on a plate. Drop the fritters into it and dust with sugar while still warm. Serve immediately.

COOK'S TIP
These rustic banana fritters are delicious with coconut or vanilla ice cream.

Per portion Energy 204Kcal/855kJ; Protein 3.9g; Carbohydrate 26.7g, of which sugars 14.8g; Fat 9.8g, of which saturates 4.4g; Cholesterol 48mg; Calcium 48mg; Fibre 1.7g; Sodium 75mg.

ROSE-FLAVOURED LASSI

Sweet and savoury lassi is always in demand at Indian and Malay coffee shops, restaurants and hawker stalls. Soothing and cooling, this Indian yogurt-based drink is an ideal partner to spicy food. Savoury lassi is often salty and flavoured with mint, whereas the sweet drink is fragrant with the traditional essences of rose or pandan leaf.

SERVES TWO

INGREDIENTS
   300ml/½ pint/1¼ cups natural
      (plain) yogurt
   5–10ml/1–2 tsp rose essence
   10ml/2 tsp sugar
   6 ice cubes, to serve
   rose petals, to decorate

1 In a jug (pitcher), beat the yogurt with 150ml/¼ pint/⅔ cup water, until smooth. Add the rose essence and sugar, adjusting the sweetness to taste, and mix well.

2 Divide the ice cubes between two glasses and pour in the lassi. Decorate with a few rose petals and serve.

Per Portion Energy 104Kcal/438kJ; Protein 7.7g; Carbohydrate 16.5g, of which sugars 16.5g; Fat 1.5g, of which saturates 0.8g; Cholesterol 2mg; Calcium 288mg; Fibre 0g; Sodium 125mg.

MANGO AND LIME LASSI

INSPIRED BY THE CLASSIC INDIAN DRINK, THIS TANGY, FRUITY BLEND IS GREAT FOR BREAKFAST OR AS A DELICIOUS PICK-ME-UP AT ANY TIME OF DAY. SOFT, RIPE MANGO BLENDED WITH YOGURT AND SHARP, ZESTY LIME AND LEMON JUICE MAKES A WONDERFULLY THICK, COOLING DRINK THAT'S PACKED WITH ENERGY. IT CAN ALSO BE ENJOYED AS A MELLOW SOOTHER WHEN YOU NEED TO UNWIND.

MAKES 2 TALL GLASSES

INGREDIENTS
    1 mango
    finely grated rind and juice of 1 lime
    15ml/1 tbsp lemon juice
    5–10ml/1–2 tsp caster
    (superfine) sugar
    100ml/3 1⁄2fl oz/scant 1⁄2 cup natural
     (plain) yogurt
    mineral water
    1 extra lime, halved, to serve

1 Peel the mango and cut the flesh from the stone (pit). Put the flesh into a blender or food processor and add the lime rind and juice.

2 Add the lemon juice, sugar and natural yogurt. Blend until the mixture is completely smooth, scraping down the sides of the bowl once or twice, if necessary. Stir in a little mineral water to thin it down.

3 Serve immediately, with half a lime on the side of each glass so that more juice can be squeezed in, if desired.

Per portion Energy 81Kcal/344kJ; Protein 3.1g; Carbohydrate 17g, of which sugars 16.7g; Fat 0.7g, of which saturates 0.4g; Cholesterol 1mg; Calcium 106mg; Fibre 2g; Sodium 43mg.

INDEX